DATE		

A Guide to
Operational
Research

A Guide to Operational Research

W.E. DUCKWORTH
Managing Director, Fulmer Research Institute

A.E. GEAR
Associate Professor in Management Studies; Deputy Dean, Faculty of Commerce, University of Aukland, New Zealand

A.G. LOCKETT
Senior Lecturer in Management Science; Dean, Faculty of Business Administration, Manchester University

LONDON
CHAPMAN AND HALL

A Halsted Press Book
JOHN WILEY & SONS, NEW YORK

First published 1962
by Methuen & Co. Ltd.
Third edition 1977
published by Chapman and Hall Ltd.
11 New Fetter Lane, London EC4P 4EE
© *1977 W.E. Duckworth, A.E. Gear, A.G. Lockett*
Typeset by Oxford Printcraft India Pvt. Ltd.
New Delhi, India.
Printed in Great Britain by
Richard Clay (The Chaucer Press) Ltd., Bungay, Suffolk

ISBN 0 412 12370 3 (cased edition)
ISBN 0 412 13500 2 (paperback edition).

Distributed in the U.S.A. by Halsted Press,
a Division of John Wiley & Sons, Inc., New York

Library of Congress Cataloging in Publication Data

Duckworth, Walter Eric.
 A guide to operational research.

 "A Halsted Press book."
 Includes bibliographies and index.
 1. Operations research. I. Gear, A.E., joint author. II. Lockett, A. Geoffrey,
joint author. III. Title. T57.6.D83   1977   001.4′24   77–4247
ISBN 0–470–99145–3

Contents

Preface

There is nothing more difficult to take in hand, more
perilous to conduct, or more uncertain in its success,
than to take the lead in the introduction of a new order of
things, because the innovator has for enemies all those
who have done well under the old conditions, and lukewarm
defenders in those who may do well under the new.

Machiavelli, The Prince

When this book was first written in 1959 I was myself a practising operational research worker in charge of a small group at the Glacier Metal Company, concerned with using Operational Research philosophy and techniques to help solve some of the managerial problems inside the company.

About that time Operational Research was beginning to attract attention in industrial circles. Many quite large research groups were being founded. The advertisement columns of the Sunday press and certain daily newspapers were full of advertisements for Operational Research practitioners, at then quite attractive salaries.

This interest by industrialists in Operational Research appeared to be based upon faith and expectation rather than upon experience. Many of the classical examples of successful Operational Research being used in the many text-books beginning to appear were still based upon the war-time experiences recently amplified in the newly released and long classified book by Waddington.*

The First International Conference on Operational Research held in 1957 attempted to restore the balance by summarizing industrial experience since the War. Even in that publication, however, many of the case studies were still incomplete, the outcomes had not yet been fully evaluated, and the many different types and levels of experience described in the proceedings of that conference did not produce a sufficiently coherent impression of post-war Operational Research practice to satisfy the busy manager, seeking a ready appreciation for his own purposes, as to whether he should seek the assistance of Operational Research.

The need for such a ready appreciation was described by the late Oscar Brandt in an editorial in his magazine *Metal Treatment* in April 1958, and it was in response to his appeal that I wrote two articles for *Metal Treatment* which appeared in September and October of that year. These subsequently

---

* References are given in alphabetical order of first author at the end of each chapter.

vii

formed the basis of the first edition of *A Guide to Operational Research* in 1962. This achieved substantially more success than I had expected, or even dreamed of, because it did provide a relatively simple coherent account by one individual of successful Operational Research being practised, albeit at a rather specialized level and not on too grand a scale, in one company.

Most of the examples were written from first-hand experience, so they possessed both an immediacy and a clarity of exposition that appeared to be lacking from many other accounts which were at second, third, and sometimes even fourth hand. There appears little doubt that the formula has been successful because after thirteen years the book was still being reprinted, it is still selling in several languages, and it has also reached the reading list of many universities and schools of management.

To be on this reading list has, in recent years, been causing me great concern because many of the illustrations of Operational Research techniques had become out of date. The book also did not describe several more modern techniques. When the book first appeared it was quite rightly criticized as providing a rather selective view of Operational Research, and as the years have gone by this criticism has become more justified.

If the book was serving a valuable purpose, as several other reviews then and subsequently have indicated, in acquainting busy managers in a readily assimilable fashion of the virtues of Operational Research, then it did seem to be a dereliction of duty to let the book die and cease publication, because there did not appear to be another book available that provided for quite the same purpose. Equally, it appeared wrong to let it continue to get more and more out of date.

The present version of the book is an attempt to resolve the dilemma with the aid of two collaborators, Tony Gear and Geoff Lockett. I did not feel capable of rewriting the book in quite the same way as sixteen years earlier because I have long ceased to be as closely connected with Operational Research practice as I was in the late 1950s. Tony Gear and Geoff Lockett are, however, such practitioners. They both benefited from reading the book in the early days. Being university teachers as well, they have a personal and a professional interest in seeing it adequately up-to-date.

We have tried in this up-dating to preserve the coherency of style that has been such a feature of the earlier book's success. However, the need for a more detailed exposition of Operational Research Techniques for the purposes of student teaching has necessitated a more mathematical, and hence more sophisticated approach to the subject. Despite this, we have endeavoured to preserve sufficient readability to enable the busy business manager to gain relatively painlessly, an understanding of what Operational Research is about. Whether or not we have succeeded is now up to you to judge.

I have taken the liberty of writing the first chapter from my own personal experience as a manager using Operational Research techniques, in the hope that it will encourage other managers to follow suit. The other chapters have been written, in the main, by one of us and then revised by the others.

W.E. Duckworth
Fulmer Research Institute Limited,
Stoke Poges

May, 1976

REFERENCES

Duckworth, W.E., *A Guide to Operational Research*, Methuen, 1962.
First International Conference on Operational Research, E.U.P., 1957.
Waddington, C.H., *Operational Research in World War II. Operational Research against the U-Boat*, Elek Science, 1973.

ACKNOWLEDGEMENTS

Much of the material used in the earlier book which was reproduced from various publications has been reprinted, and permission for its use is gratefully acknowledged. New material from *Technological Forecasting in Perspective* by Jansch, the Open University and *The Limits to Growth* by Meadows and colleagues has been incorporated and permission for its inclusion is also gratefully acknowledged.

Many thanks are also due to many colleagues, especially D.G.S. Davies, who read the manuscript critically and helpfully and contributed to Chapter 8, and to Mr. R.F. Flint who helped to prepare the index.

Finally, but by no means minimally, we owe much gratitude to Mrs. Joan Tarrant who typed an incredible number of scripts with patience and fortitude.

1 What Operational Research Is and Does

Operational Research is the art of winning wars without actually fighting.

Arthur Clarke

What Operational Research is

Operational Research (O.R.) has never been an easy subject to define, comprising as it does the application of several scientific disciplines to the solving of complex problems in the management of human affairs. The Operational Research Society of the United Kingdom have the following official definition: 'Operational Research is the application of the methods of science to complex problems arising in the direction and management of large systems of men, machines, materials, and money in industry, business, government, and defence. The distinctive approach is to develop a scientific model of the system, incorporating measurements of factors such as chance and risk, with which to predict and compare the outcomes of alternative decisions, strategies, or controls. The purpose is to help management determine its policy and actions scientifically'. At the time of producing this definition there were some 38 others which all have merit, and no doubt there have been many more produced since. I myself prefer to regard Operational Research as the study of administrative systems pursued in the same scientific manner in which systems in physics, chemistry, and biology are studied in the natural sciences.

The problem of definition really arises because language is a classification process and the more complex a process becomes the less easy it is to define it in language which can convey a roughly similar meaning to all its readers. The more precise such a definition is in describing particular attributes of Operational Research the more it can be resented by the physicist, the mathematician, the economist, the sociologist, the work-study man, etc. as encroaching on their particular preserve. It is quite true that O.R. does encroach on these preserves but if it is any consolation to the gamekeepers it is a poacher that treats many such preserves with the same indifference to plunder and ought to continue to do so.

A further problem of definition is that, while it is often easy to describe a profession or trade in terms of the tools used (there is for instance little problem in understanding the role of the electron microscopist or the X-ray crystallographer), any definition which so illuminates Operational Research tends to give the impression that it is just a rag-bag of techniques.

It is, of course, more than this but every discipline must have techniques to implement its means of operation, and to describe Operational Research without describing techniques would be to attempt to describe a scent without ever having experienced one. A third major problem of definition is that, since Operational Research covers a very wide embracing field of human management, it is sometimes hard to attempt to describe it in these terms without appearing to usurp the function of management itself.

This is one of the major problems which Operational Research implementation has had to face since its inception. It seemed at one time that the exigencies of war had helped to solve this problem, and those responsible for executing decisions had a close rapport with those responsible for understanding and analysing the decisions to be implemented. Waddington's recent book, referenced in the Preface, suggests however that, even under the pressure of survival against the U-boat, the problems of relationships between the managers and operational research workers were just as difficult as they have been ever since.

It is very important for the health of industry that this problem of relationships should be solved. This is one of the main motivating forces behind the rewriting of this book. It is a very understandable problem. The decision maker has to make the decisions. If some other agent analyses, inter-prets, and resolves them into components and alternatives, what is there still left for the decision maker to do? There is a great deal. The analysis of decisions by even the most skilled practitioners who have not the responsibi-lity for making them and for 'carrying the can' still lacks some indefinable quality; let us call it judgement.

It is this judgement that finally makes the decision viable or otherwise. It is this judgement for which people are paid high salaries.

They are not paid for the quantity of work they do. They are not paid high salaries for the amount of time and effort they put into their decisions. They are paid, as Elliot Jaques has shown, for the quality of their decisions and for the length of time which has to elapse before the validity of these decisions can be demonstrated. It is therefore surely more important that the decision maker should have the most valuable aids to his decision making that he can obtain. The manager does not however just want masses and masses of information. It is a standard joke among the uninitiated in management practice to jibe at the manager who says 'I must make a decision, do not confuse me with facts'. Unfortunately, too many managers do mistake facts for analysis and find that they are faced with a completely undigestible volume of information.

This makes it almost impossible for them to make a proper decision because, although they may consider by using their judgement that a particular course of action is the right one, they feel that it is inappropriate to take that course of action until they have checked it against the available information. Because this is too big a task to undertake in the time, they remain like hypnotized rabbits until the effective time for a decision has passed and circumstances take over.

What Operational Research can do is to analyse the available information, not just from the point of view of the economist, or the physicist, or the management scientist, or the production engineer but, with true scientific objectivity, to sort out which information is relevant, to sort out which information from past experience has a causal relationship with the situation being examined, to identify where information does not exist so that at least its absence can be noted if it cannot be rectified, and then to attempt to illustrate the likely outcomes of certain courses of action based upon the information analysed, and only on the information analysed.

The objective of the study is to gain understanding of administrative systems so that they may be more readily controlled, just as systems in the natural sciences are more readily controlled than they were and can in fact be harnessed to man's uses. Incidentally, the word 'control' is used throughout this book in the regulative and not the restrictive sense.

We can now switch on an electric light with a good degree of probability that the bulb will light up. We can spray crops against certain diseases with a strong expectation that protection will be assured without the occurrence of unforeseen side-effects. But can the average manager be as sure of the workings of his administrative system?

Can a manager reduce his stocks to a particular level and be sure that he will not endanger his productive processes or let his customers down? Can he change his distributive outlets and know that he will be better off? Can he in fact introduce changes in routine and procedure without considerable uncertainty as to their results?

Does a manager know very often whether a change is necessary or even desirable? Modern industry is so complex that the optimum point of operation of many of its systems is no longer within the intuitive comprehension of individuals.

To enable this intuition, this imaginative judgement, which is at the core of management to hold its rightful place in the controlling of such systems is the function of O.R. Its job is to study these systems and to understand how they may be controlled by simple rules. Managers often feel that scientific methods are a threat to their intuition, but I hope to show that the opposite is true.

If you doubt the ability of simple rules to handle complex situations, consider how the simple rule 'drive on the left' prevented chaos on the roads of Britain in the early days of motoring. The equally simple rule 'no right turn across a stream of traffic in cities' has also eased the traffic flow in our towns considerably. Instead of holding up traffic as shown in Fig. 1.1 (a), drivers keep turning left until they can cross the traffic steam at right-angles as shown in Fig. 1.1 (b). Many junctions controlled by traffic lights now handle traffic more rapidly than they used to.

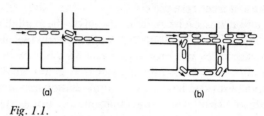

(a)   (b)

Fig. 1.1.

Other recent examples of how simple rules can influence highly complex situations have been provided by the 1973 oil crisis.

The reduction of speed limits in most countries reduced accident rates by between 25% and 50%. Although analysis of accidents has never established a causal relationship between speed and accidents, the application of a simple rule to reduce speed limits has had a striking effect on accidents. The experience of Sweden in imposing severe speed limits after the change from left-hand driving to right-hand driving in 1967 had the same effect.

The second striking example from the oil crisis was the simple solution found in Britain to reduce the queues for petrol at garages. When the rule changed from a £1 maximum purchase to a £1 minimum purchase the queues almost disappeared because motorists who were stopping frequently to keep their tanks filled up were obviously not prepared to pay £1 each time for just a gallon or two of petrol (this of course was before the subsequent price rise).

By studying such examples and finding simple keys to unlock complex situations, Operational Research can add greatly to the armoury of weapons at a manager's disposal.

In summary, the purpose of Operational Research is to help managers to make decisions. It is to provide an objective analysis of the situation and a critical evaluation of the alternatives by using any type of experience in any discipline with some pretentions to scientific rigour and objectivity. The scarcest commodity in industry is judgement; let us not use it trivially.

What Operational Research does

Given that there is a system which may not be operating in an optimum manner, what can O.R. do? What does O.R. bring to the situation which Work Study, Management Accounting, and the rest do not bring? After all, although these techniques do not usually look at the system as a whole, and are not usually required to, there seems to be no reason why they should not do so. In that event, of course, one may ask what O.R. brings to the situation that the intelligent manager, who is always trying to look at the system as a whole, does not bring.

To answer this question it is probably useful to go a little into the history of O.R. Although (if one really tried) one could probably discover elements of O.R. in the military work of Archimedes and some of the scientists who worked for Napoleon, and certainly of some of the scientists in World War I, it was really in World War II that it began to establish itself as a separate discipline.

When the British Government, anxious not to waste resources in the years of total war following Dunkirk, banded together groups of scientists to assist field commanders in solving strategic and tactical problems, it caused biologists to examine problems in electronics, physicists to observe movements of men rather than movements of molecules, mathematicians to examine how probability theory could influence men's survival, and chemists to study equilibria in systems other than chemical ones. Similar work was being done under the Chief Scientist of the U.S. War Department.

From all this work there arose the realization that techniques for studying systems in one discipline could be used with success in solving problems in systems outside the discipline.

Communication within a command or a unit exhibited symptoms similar to those that had been studied in telephone circuits. The control of an operation involving men and machines needed the same requirements for its success as did the servo-mechanisms of an aircraft. The delays in unloading ships at ports were similar to the delays in waiting for calls at telephone exchanges, which had been studied for many years.

All these and other examples showed that there was a need for a technology in the study of systems which could draw from experience in the biological, physical, chemical, and engineering sciences and utilize this experience in a wider sphere. This common technology is the technology of O.R.

One characteristic of O.R. therefore is that it is inter-disciplinary. It draws on techniques from biology, physics, chemistry, mathematics, economics, and so on, and distils from them those that apply in the system being studied. Thus it is not surprising to find in an O.R. team men who have qualified in many different subjects and who can share their experience in pursuit of a common aim.

I must be careful, however, to avoid giving the impression that O.R. is techniques-bound, or that it searches around for a known poultice to clap on a management ache. This is becoming more and more true of many situations. This book will describe many techniques which can be applied, with modification, in well known types of problem with a good chance of success.

But this is not the whole of O.R. Above all, O.R. is an attitude of mind. It is the attitude of mind of an enquiring scientist who is not content to accept a system as it is, but who wants to analyse it, find out what makes it tick, see how it responds to stimuli, and encourage it to evolve in the best direction.

In the best O.R. work the technique for solving the problem arises from a study of the problem and may become a new technique to be added to those in the O.R. worker's locker for use in similar problems elsewhere. With the other management aids the techniques for solving particular problems have usually been standardized and do not need to be developed during the course of an investigation.

This description of O.R. may send a shiver down the spine of many a manager. A manager has to operate his systems willy-nilly. Work must be carried out, and goods produced, despatched, sold, and paid for. This usually needs the full-time attention of a competent staff, comfortable in the working of an established procedure, knowing all the snags, confident in the way in which other people's work fits into their own. If some crazy scientist comes monkeying around with this scheme, what is going to happen? The basis of all scientific work is experimentation. Experimentation is just what apparently cannot be done with administrative systems.

The resolution of this impasse is a major conceptual contribution of O.R. This is the second hurdle over which I and my readers must leap. The first, if you remember, is that O.R. does not deprive managers of discretion; it frees them for higher levels of judgement. The second is that O.R. does not experiment with the system itself; it experiments with a model of the system.

This concept of model is very important and I will elaborate on it. By 'model' is meant not necessarily a physical representation of the system such as a scale model which architects may make before finalizing the design of a building. The model in O.R. may be a mathematical formula or some other abstract representation which behaves in a similar way to the system being studied. Let me give a very simple example of a mathematical model.

Suppose you are throwing a party and have £100 to spend. Then whatever you spend on food and on drink must not total more than £100. If you spend £60 on food you cannot spend more than £40 on drink, and so on. The mathematical model for this is:

$$x + y \leq 100$$

where x and y are the amounts, in pounds, spent on food and drink respectively, and the symbol $\leq$ means 'less than or equal to'. Thus if x is £20, y must be less than or equal to £80, and so on. The model $x + y \leq 100$ not only expresses the system you are examining more concisely than can be done in words, but it has the same properties and can be experimented on. You can say: 'If I spend £40 on food (x) then I cannot spend more than

£60 on drink (*y*)'. This is a simpler method of exploring the situation than actually spending £40 on food and finding that you had only £60 left for drink.

You might say that this is just simple arithmetic and that no mathematical model is needed, but stop and think. When you are using simple arithmetic you are still using a model of the situation. Because you think in terms of pounds and pence in working out your change from the tobacconist or calculating if you can afford a holiday in Spain you are not actually dealing in pounds and pence. You do not have the money in your hand to count out. You are using a model to explore different possibilities of the real situation and then choosing the best result.

Very often the result is not what the model predicted. I would like to meet the genius whose holiday cost him just what he thought it would, but unless things went drastically wrong and some important factor was missed out of the model, such as the air fare or the cost of living abroad, then there is no doubt that the model was useful and even necessary in coming to a decision.

The advantage of the model $x + y \leq 100$ over simple arithmetic is that more complex variations may be introduced and analysed readily. Suppose you did not want to spend more than £100 and yet the drink must cost twice as much as the food. The model of this situation is provided by the simultaneous expressions:

$$x + y \leq 100$$

$$y = 2x$$

This situation can then be analysed readily to reveal that *x* must lie between 0 and £33.33, and *y* must be double whatever *x* is. You then know that, with the conditions you have stated, you cannot spend more than £33.33 on food. This kind of model, on a more elaborate scale, is used in linear programming.

This is the way an O.R. team works. It studies the situation, constructs a model of the system (usually mathematical or of similar abstraction), experiments on it to find the optimum performance, and recommends this to the manager. He may then be reluctant to implement a change because the model is more complicated and hence less easy to understand than the simple accounting arithmetic that we are all used to, or because the more complex the real system the less likely it is that the model can represent it exactly, or because the consequences of making a bad change in a system are often very serious.

This is very natural. This is why O.R. workers must take great pains to explain their work. This is why O.R. men must often be content to tackle simple problems until their ability to construct a viable model and produce the correct results from experiments on it has gained the confidence of their superiors and colleagues. When this stage has been reached, and men in charge of enterprises feel able to examine some of their most complex systems and explore the possibilities of their evolution with a hitherto unknown and unexpected freedom, the fruits of such endeavour can be very great.

I must not leave the impression that O.R. has a message only for managers. It also has a message for Work Study men, Industrial Engineers, Management Accountants, and other staff functionaries. Operational Research, as its name implies, is research. Its practitioners are constantly seeking new ways of analysing situations and understanding systems. Some of the techniques they evolve should properly be incorporated into the body of knowledge of the other disciplines. Some very good examples of how this may be achieved are contained in *Operational Research and the Social Sciences* published by Tavistock Publications in 1966.

Work Study is beginning to make effective use of statistical methods, Management Accounting can fruitfully employ linear programming, and Industrial Engineers are finding queueing theory of considerable assistance. This is as it should be. All will profit if workers in these fields regard O.R. not as a rival but as a partner and a source of refreshment.

The benefits of Operational Research

When this book was first written I had personal experience of many operational research techniques but always from the point of view of the operational research worker putting forward these ideas to management. For the past eight years I have been the Chief Executive of a commercial company engaged in contract research, testing and consultancy, in a highly competitive national and international field. There may be many managers who do not consider that contract research is an industrial activity similar to that of manufacturing motor cars or making soap powder etc., and who therefore may not consider that experience in running a contract research organization is relevant to the problems of running other types of industrial activity.

There are probably arguments on both sides. There is more uncertainty in selling contract research than there is in selling motor cars, washing machines, soap powders, etc. People need motor cars, soap powders, washing machines, etc., but they do not always need the services of a contract research organization. They may have their own extensive research activities. They may not be interested in new ideas, which are really what a contract research organization sells. Hence, some of the Operational Research techniques which enable one to deal with situations of uncertainty will have more relevance (and they certainly have had relevance in my experience) to a contract research organization than they have to the more traditional types of manufacturing activity. On the other hand, successful contract research relationships are just as enduring as those between a major manufacture and its established suppliers.

However since all the normal business problems of employing people, managing them, providing job satisfaction, ensuring adequate cash flow, compiling profit and loss accounts, etc. apply to contract research as to any other business, it is probable that my direct experience is sufficiently relevant to make it worthwhile recounting the use I have made of Operational Research techniques as a manager for the past seven years.

In what way do I consider that Operational Research has benefited the Fulmer Research Institute while I have been Chief Executive? It is always impossible to separate completely cause and effect in such a complicated process as running a company. In describing the ways that the Institute has grown in eight years I do not want to imply that this has been primarily or even secondarily due to the use of certain Operational Research concepts and techniques.

I have been blessed with many hard-working, imaginative, courageous, and skilful colleagues. I have been fortunate in having an understanding Board of Directors who have cushioned me from some of my worst mistakes. I have been especially blessed with a Chairman whose powers of judgement exceed my own and who has warned me of pitfalls before I have seen them myself and therefore given me more time than I unaided would have had to avoid them. The Institute has a clientele of both large and small firms who have an excellent relationship with it.

All these factors have influenced the growth of the organization but Operational Research concepts and techniques have certainly contributed and it would be wrong to ignore their impact. In describing where I feel they have had this impact I am suggesting to other managers that, although they would not be a panacea, they may have a similar effect in their own companies.

The ability to deal in a quantitative manner with situations of uncertainty is one of the most powerful contributions of O.R. In the first edition of this book I emphasized Bertrand Russell's dictum that we are not able to predict the future with complete certainty but equally we are not entirely uncertain about the future. One factor in helping the Fulmer Research Institute's income to grow some five-fold over eight years has been the technique of forecasting contract research income. This helped to predict cash flow and enable decisions to be taken in advance about the purchase of equipment etc.

The forecasting of contract research income is a more complex operation than the simple extrapolation used for normal sales forecasting. The number of potential clients is relatively limited. The number of subjects on which they might seek the services of the Institute is restricted. The time-scale over which the decision to use the Institute's services is taken is substantial and the sums of money involved are relatively large. The selling techniques used in contract research are entirely different from those for normal goods.

One has to identify the particular need of the customer for a particular research, to show how it opens up opportunities for him or helps to solve existing problems, and to satisfy him not only that the Institute has the necessary facilities and staff to carry out the research but also that it has the right kind of ideas and the ability to carry through each competent research programme at least as efficiently, and if possible more efficiently, than he can do it himself. Therefore, the forecasting of contract research income has to be done on an individually identifiable basis, much more so than is the case with the more typical forecasting examples dealt with later in the book.

The idea of individual forecasting on a systematic scale was entirely new to the Institute and so it can legitimately be said to be an Operational Research technique brought in from outside. There had been individual spot forecasts made in a rather random fashion by particular individuals within the organization, and this experience was helpful since it meant that several key members of staff responded readily to a more systematic approach.

This is a very important ingredient of successful implementation of Operational Research techniques and one to be looked at closely by the appropriate manager and Operational Research worker. If the climate and experience within the firm is entirely wrong for the type of quantitative approach being studied, then it is likely to make slow progress. If, however, there have already been rudimentary attempts by particular individuals to solve their own problems by applying some quantitative approach, then their reception is likely to be much more friendly and cooperative. It is probably better to try to seed some ideas in particular places and see how they flourish initially than to try to drive them through in a sledge hammer approach.

Therefore, in saying that the systematic technique of contract income forecasting was an Operational Research technique introduced from outside, I must acknowledge that the previous experience and attempts of the existing staff to provide their own estimates of future income were a great help in the speedy implementation of the technique.

The need for forecasting can be illustrated dramatically. At any time the existing research contracts within the Institute have a further expected time span of between one month and two years. If, at any time, no new contracts were to be negotiated between the Institute and its clients, the contract income profile of the Institute would appear as shown by the full line in Fig. 1.2.

It will be seen that future income decreases to a low level within six months. This is confirmed by the observation that the outstanding sum on contracts to be completed is about half the annual contract research expenditure of the Institute. In other words, the order book is of about six months duration.

Since the profit margin on contract research is necessarily very slender because of the highly competitive nature of the business, it will be clear that

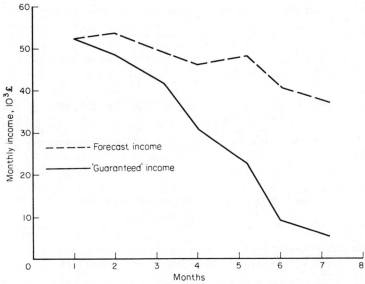

Fig. 1.2. Expected monthly contract income of the Fulmer Research Institute; full line, guaranteed income; dashed line, forecast income.

any progression along the curve shown in Fig. 1.2 for more than two months would place the Institute in a difficult financial position. It may strike many managers accustomed to the more secure trading in motor cars, soap pow— ders, etc. that this is a rather knife-edge situation which they would find uncomfortable. It is this knife-edge attribute of contract research which encourages me to believe that we are in as big a commercial jungle as anybody else and hence that our experiences are relevant and purposeful.

Let us return to the forecasting. At any time a substantial number of contracts is in process of negotiation, and also some of the ongoing contracts have a chance of renewal at the end of their present term. This is because some contracts last for either six months or a year and if satisfactory progress has been made at the end of that time, and the outcome of the research is showing sufficient promise, a renewal can be obtained. At any time the con— tract sums being negotiated are known, and the probability of either a suc— cessful new contract or a contract renewal can also be estimated. Hence the contract forecast can be prepared in the style shown in Table 1.1.

It might seem that the concept of probability of obtaining contracts must be rather strange because in the event one either gets or does not get one, so the ultimate assessment of probability is either 0 or 1. If one takes any indi— vidual group of contracts for a particular research group, and if all the con— tracts under negotiation are given a probability of, say, 0.7, then what it means is that the group expects 70% of the present contracts it is negotiating to be successful.

Table 1.1.　Example of contract research forecast.

	Four-weekly months													
	1	2	3	4	5	6	7	8	9	10	11	12	13	*Notes*
Existing contract No.	INCOME IN POUNDS													
478	800	200	—	—	720	720	720	720	720	720	720	720	720	(1)
		(Delay period)												
501	150	150	150	150	150	150	150	150	150	150	150	150	150	(2)
516	1100	1100	1100	1100	1100	1100	↑550	550	550	550	550	550	550	(3)
						RENEWAL								
New contracts expected														
601		1000	1000	1000	1000	1000	1000	1000	1000	1000	—	—	—	(4)
602					600	600	600							(5)

Notes:
(1) Probability of renewal is 0.9 (2) Continuing contract (3) Probability of renewal is 0.5
(4) £10 000 contract, probability is 0.9 (5) £3000 contract, probability is 0.6.

The success of the forecasting technique cannot be assessed by taking individual contracts and seeing whether the 0.7 probability was achieved for that contract because in the event it was either 0 or 1. However, by multiplying the expected contract income by the expected probability and summing these over a group of contracts, one is able to determine over a period the expected new contract income. By adding this expected new contract income to the curve shown in Fig. 1.2 for the existing contract income, one is able to establish a new curve for expected total contract income over a given period shown by the broken line.

This may seem a somewhat uncertain process, since it also has to include an estimate of the time at which new contracts are achieved, because the income does not materialize until the contract negotiations are complete. When there are sufficient new contracts under negotiation the disappointments and the successes average out in such a way that over the many years during which the system has been operating at Fulmer the comparison of expected contract income with actual contract income is as shown in Fig. 1.3.

The agreement on the whole is extremely good. It has certainly been sufficient for the Company to plan its own future with confidence. It has not always been so good as to throw doubt upon whether the technique has any real meaning, because, as is shown, there have been periods when the actual contract income has fallen substantially for a short period below that expected. These have been circumstances of semi-crisis within the Institute.

If these crises had not occurred, I think it would have been appropriate to say that the Institute's income is sufficiently stable and assured for it not to need a forecasting technique.

The general accuracy of the relationship shows just how valid is the application of the principles of mathematical statistics (to be discussed in Chapter
2) to this situation of extreme individual uncertainty. There are many other
such situations in industry where it may seem absurd to prophesy because of
extreme individual uncertainties, but when many of these individual uncertainties are aggregated the results can be extremely satisfying and helpful
to management.

The principles of project planning described in Chapter 8 have also worked
very successfully at Fulmer. Knowledge of several other techniques described
in this book have proved valuable in particular circumstances. Queuing
theory (Chapter 3) has helped in planning the telephone system at Fulmer:
only incoming calls are now routed through an operator/receptionist, and
almost all outgoing calls are made directly through a level 9 access system.

This was decided after it had been shown that when external calls made by
inside staff were routed through the operator there was a significant risk of
external callers not being able to get through in the kind of time for which
external callers are prepared to wait. Also, at times when the operator was
busy with external calls urgent outside calls required by members of staff

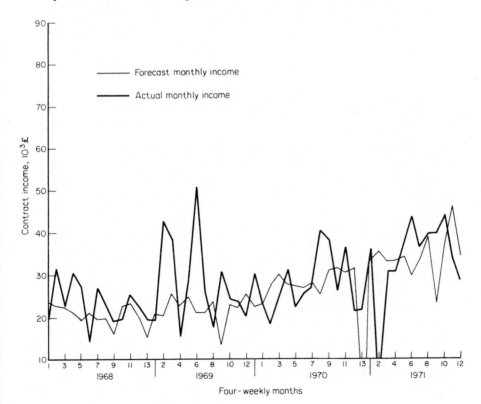

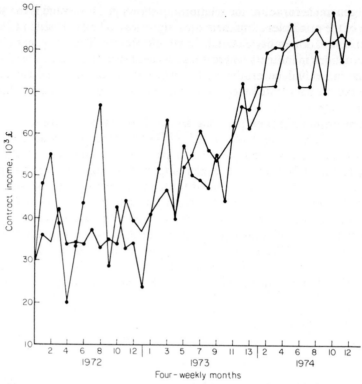

Fig. 1.3. Comparison of expected contract income with actual contract income.

could not be made, so there was a substantial loss of internal efficiency. With the present system the staff has doubled and yet external calls are made more swiftly and external callers rarely have to complain of not having an almost immediate reply. There is still only one telephone operator.

Monte Carlo methods (Chapter 5) prove of great value in carrying out random checks on the utilization of particular pieces of apparatus to help assess whether cases which are submitted from time to time for duplication or re-purchase or up-dating the apparatus are justified in terms of the expected use of the equipment.

In the manufacturing activities carried out by Fulmer, although again these are of a relatively simple nature, some stock control methods used in O.R. (Chapter 6) have proved of value.

Decision theory concepts (Chapter 9) have been of major assistance at some critical times in the Company's recent history, notably when it has had to purchase major pieces of apparatus, to enter new business, or to remain competitive in existing businesses. They have also been helpful when bids have been made for some Companies which have recently joined the Group.

I hope that sufficient has now been said to show how I, as a practising executive with Operational Research experience, have found general Operational Research concepts of great value in running a Company which has shown above average growth compared with the rest of British industry, which has expanded its overseas operations quite considerably, and which has maintained profitability in circumstances where cash flow needs have required substantial bank borrowing and hence incurred the penalty of high rates of interest.

The purpose of this book is to convince other managers that Operational Research can assist them in the same way.

W.E.D.

REFERENCES

Jaques, Elliott, *Measurement of Responsibility*, Tavistock Publications, 1956.

BIBLIOGRAPHY

Churchman, C.W., Ackoff, R.L. and Arnoff, E.L., *Introduction to Operations Research*, Wiley, 1957.
McCloskey, J.F. and Trefethen, F.N., *Operations Research for Management*, Part I, Johns Hopkins Press, 1954.
McCloskey, J.F. and Coppinger, J.M., *Operations Research for Management*, Part II, Johns Hopkins Press, 1956.

A comprehensive list of recent books and articles on O.R. can be obtained from the U.K. Operational Research Society.

2 Measuring Uncertainty

When you can measure what you are speaking of and express it in numbers you know that on which you are discoursing. But when you cannot measure it and express it in numbers, your knowledge is of a very meagre and unsatisfactory kind.

Lord Kelvin

Assembly of Data

In Chapter 1 we demonstrated the value of being able to assemble data on individual contracts, each of which had a high degree of uncertainty, in a coherent way so as to produce an income forecast of substantial reliability. This is only one example of the way in which information arising in commercial or production operations, however unreliable or variable it may seem at first glance, can be collected and presented to provide information from which useful and correct decisions can be made. Since this collection and presentation of information in a systematic way is fundamental to all Operational Research procedures, some of the methods of doing this, derived from mathematical statistics, are presented in this chapter.

The simplest way to systematize data is to collect it in a tabular or a graphical form. For example, the daily output from a production plant may be as shown in Table 2.1.

Table 2.1. Daily output from a production plant.

Day number	1	2	3	4	5	6	7	8	9	10	etc.
Tonnage	30.3	15.2	18.1	20.9	32.4	33.7	30.0	27.8	25.6	31.5	

It will be noticed that there is a substantial variation in the daily tonnage from 15.2 to 33.7. There may be well known reasons for this variation; it may be connected with deliveries of raw materials, variation in production orders, breakdowns, or low efficiency of operation. If however there are no known causes for particular variations, it is useful to assemble the data first in tabular and then in diagrammatic form. Table 2.2 shows how the data can be presented in ranges of production tonnage, and then this table can be converted into the type of diagram shown in Fig. 2.1 known as a histogram. Table 2.2 and Fig. 2.1 assume more data than in Table 2.1.

Table 2.2. **Summary.**

Range of production tonnage	11–15+	16–20+	21–25+	26–30+	31–35	etc.
Number of occurrences	1	3	3	6	4	

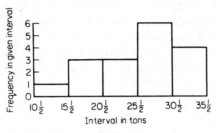

Fig. 2.1. Histogram of output tonnages.

Histograms are very useful because they begin to show immediately whether the data are subject to random fluctuations or to specific variations with clear and positive causes. A typical random histogram is shown in Fig. 2.2 for the heights of males in the United Kingdom.

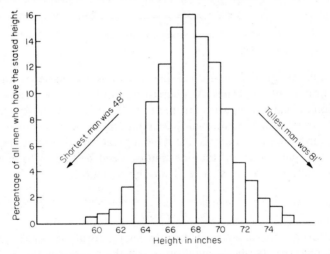

Fig. 2.2. Heights of males in the United Kingdom.

Several thousand men were measured and found to have heights varying between 4 feet and 6 ft 9 in. The histogram was constructed by dividing the measurements into seventeen intervals, one inch apart, and counting the number of men whose heights lay within each interval. Thus there may be 520 men whose heights are between 5 ft 6 in and just less than 5 ft 7 in, 870 men whose heights are between 5 ft 7 in and just less than 5 ft 8 in, etcetera.

The Normal Distribution

If the intervals in a histogram are made sufficiently short, and if the size of the population is large enough, a smooth curve such as that shown in Fig. 2.3 is obtained. This smooth curve is known as the frequency curve of the variable, i.e. the height of males in the UK. It turns out to often be the case that when a frequency curve is plotted in practice the shape is that of a 'bell' (Fig. 2, 3). This curve approximates to a mathematically defined form known as the normal distribution. This distribution is of great importance and plays a central role in mathematical statistics. It has useful properties which enable valuable conclusions to be drawn from collected data, even though, as has been said, individual figures contributing to the data are subject to considerable variability.

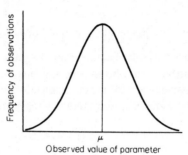

Fig. 2.3.

A particular feature of the normal distribution is its symmetry, and this is one of its important properties. Any departure from symmetry in a particular distribution indicates a departure from normality which can have interesting consequences from an Operational Research point of view.

Another important property is that it has a precise mathematical equation, and only two parameters of the distribution need be known to enable the entire distribution to be constructed from this equation:

$$f(x) = \frac{1}{\sigma\sqrt{(2\pi)}}\, e^{(x-\mu)^2/2\sigma^2}$$

These parameters are the average (mean) which is given the Greek symbol μ, and the spread (or standard deviation) given the Greek symbol σ. The expression $f(x)$ is the relative frequency of the value occurring, or more correctly $f(x)dx$ is the relative frequency of x taking values in the interval from x to $(x + dx)$.

The average is a well known concept and it is sufficient to remind readers that it is the sum of the observations divided by the total number of observations. The average of a normal distribution is the mid-point of the distribution shown in Fig. 2.3. The concept of standard deviation is not so familiar and needs some explanation. It is a measure of the spread of the information. If the two distributions shown in Fig. 2.4 are compared they are seen to have the same average but their width, or spread, is very different. This means that their standard deviations are also very different. Curve A has a much smaller standard deviation than curve B.

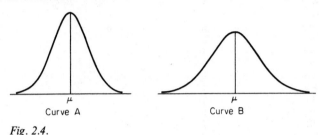

Fig. 2.4.

The mathematical definition of the standard deviation is that it is the root mean square of the deviations from the average. This is calculated as follows. Each observation in the population is subtracted from the mean, the result is squared (this removes the minus signs which arise when the observations are greater than the mean), these squares are added together, divided by the total number of observations, and then the square root of the final answer is taken. Two examples of this process are given below.

Example 1

Suppose a large number of Vickers hardness measurements have been taken on a block of steel for standardization purposes. The mean of this very large number of observations is 500 V.D.H. and this can be taken as the 'true' mean of the population. The scatter of some observations about this mean is shown in the first column of Table 2.3. In the second column the difference between these observations and the mean is given, and in the third column this figure is squared.

The total of column (3) is 41. The total number of observations in the sample is 17, and thus the mean square deviation, which is the sum of (observation − true mean)^2 divided by the total number of observations, is 41/17 or 2.41.

The square root of 2.41 is 1.55 and this is the standard deviation of the observations about their true mean. In some statistical calculations, the square of the standard deviation, in this case 2.4, is used. This is known as the variance.

Example 2

Let us suppose a year's daily scrap figures have been analysed and found to follow a normal distribution; 250 figures are usually sufficient for this

Table 2.3.

(1) Observation V.D.H.	(2) Observation minus true mean	(3) (Observation minus true mean)^2
501	1	1
503	3	9
500	0	0
498	−2	4
499	−1	1
502	2	4
500	0	0
499	−1	1
501	1	1
500	0	0
501	1	1
498	−2	4
499	−1	1
502	2	4
497	−3	9
500	0	0
501	1	1

purpose. The 'true mean as defined above was 10.3%. Typical daily figures are shown in column (1) of Table 2.4; column (2) is again the deviation from the mean, and column (3) is the square of this deviation.

Table 2.4.

(1) Observation %	(2) Deviation from mean	(3) (Deviation)^2
12.3	2.0	4.00
11.5	1.2	1.44
10.6	0.3	0.09
8.7	−1.6	2.56
13.6	3.3	10.89
7.8	−2.5	6.25
13.5	3.2	10.24
12.0	1.7	2.89
11.1	0.8	0.64
10.7	0.4	0.16
11.3	1.0	1.00
9.5	−0.8	0.64
12.9	2.6	6.76
11.1	0.8	0.64
10.3	0	0
12.6	2.3	5.29
9.8	−0.5	0.25
10.6	0.3	0.09
9.2	−1.1	1.21
10.8	0.5	0.25
10.9	0.6	0.36

The total of column (3) is 55.65, the total number of observations in the sample is 21, and hence the mean square deviation is 55.65/21, or 2.65. The square root of 2.65 is 1.63 which is therefore the standard deviation of the listed observations about their true mean. The variance is, of course, 2.65.

In actual calculations for a normal distribution all the observations would of course be included. These examples are therefore purely illustrative at this stage.

The standard deviation is very useful because, as has been said above, when the mean and the standard deviation of a normal distribution are known, the distribution is uniquely defined. One very valuable property of the normal distribution is that the proportion of observations lying within a given number of standard deviations from the mean can be precisely determined. This arises from the fact that the equation of the normal distribution is uniquely determined from the mean and the standard deviation.

To give some actual values, approximately two-thirds of all the observations in a normal distribution lie in the range of the average ± 1 standard deviation. Nearly 95% lie within the range of the mean ± 2 standard deviations, and about 99.7% lie within the range of the mean ± 3 standard deviations. This is illustrated diagrammatically in Fig. 2.5.

In the original example of the heights of males in the U.K. the average height was 5 ft 7 in and the standard deviation was 2.5 in, so 99.7% of the

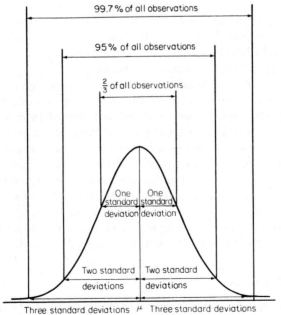

Fig. 2.5. Normal distribution and standard deviation.

observations lay within the range of 4 ft $11^1/_2$ in to 6 ft $2^1/_2$ in (5 ft 7 in $\pm$ 3 × 2.5 in).

If all that you knew about a certain man was that he was only 4 ft 3 in tall it would be most unlikely that he was a full-grown Englishman because the chances of his being so are less than one in a thousand. Less than one in a thousand Englishmen, according to the properties of the normal distribution, are less than 4 ft $11^1/_2$ in tall when fully grown. If you received more data about the men from the same town as the original one and found that they were all below 4 ft $11^1/_2$ in, your conviction would become increasingly strong that these men were not Englishmen. Similarly, if you had been purchasing steel for many years from a particular supplier and found that the tensile strength was 30 tons/in^2 and the standard deviation 0.5 tons/in^2, then if you were offered some steel with a tensile strength of only 28 tons/in^2, which it was claimed was the same steel that you had been buying for so long, you would have every reason to be sceptical about the claim.

Examples 1 and 2 show how the proportions in Fig. 2.5 operate with the quite small samples to be discussed again later. In Example 2 the population true mean is 10.3% and the standard deviation 1.63%. The range of the mean $\pm$ one standard deviation is thus 11.93 to 8.67, and 14 of the 21 observations, or two-thirds, lie within this range. The range of the mean $\pm$ two standard deviations is 13.56 to 7.04. Only 1 of the 21 observations, or 5%, lies outside these limits. In Example 1, the one standard deviation limits (often called 'one sigma limits' after the Greek letter σ, used for population standard deviation) are 501.55 to 498.45; 12 out of 17 observations lie within these limits. The 'two sigma limits' are 503.1 and 496.9. None of the 17 observations lies outside these limits, although two are very near.

When the properties of the normal distribution of a given sample of data drawn from a complete bank of data called a population are known, it is possible to determine whether or not fresh observations belong to that population with a given level of confidence defined as a probability. By determining the means and standard deviations of the populations from which the two sets of numbers are drawn it can be assessed whether they are from the same population or not. If the probability is high that they are not, then there must be an underlying reason for this and understanding of this reason may be valuable. On the other hand if the two sets of observations do not differ greatly, and can reasonably be assumed to belong to the same population, it would probably be a waste of effort to investigate further such differences as do exist, as they can be attributed to chance.

Probability Estimates

Calculations based upon observations from these distributions enable the Operational Research worker to say, for example, whether observations obtained in real life, or in an experiment on a model, really show that things have been changed, or whether what was thought to be an important result could actually have occurred by chance because of the inherent uncertainty. Here we are making statements in probabilistic terms, but most of us are familiar anyway with the ideas of probability. In tossing coins one expects heads and tails to occur with equal frequency, so we say that the probability of a head or a tail is $1/2$. In throwing an ordinary die we can see that the chance of getting any particular number at the first throw is 1 in 6. If a penny always came down heads or a die always came down with the five uppermost it would not take many throws before we began to suspect that all was not as it should be.

We would probably doubt the genuineness of the penny after five heads had occurred in the first five throws. Calculation shows that this sequence of heads could occur by chance once in thirty-two times, so it is not completely out of the question that the penny is unbiased. A probability of 1/32 is small enough, however, to make us suspicious. If we threw the penny another five times and had a further five heads then we would have no doubt that the penny was biased, because 10 heads in a row occur by chance only 1 in 1024 times and we all know from our experience with football pools that this kind of chance event does not happen to us, because these odds are similar to those of winning a worthwhile dividend in any one year.

Mathematical statistics provides means of calculating the probability of chance events in situations much more complicated than those of tossing pennies or throwing dice.

The example in Table 2.5 illustrates this. Suppose the daily output of two particular machines varied over a period in the way indicated. The output of the first machine was higher than that of the second, but can we be sure that if further observations were taken the difference would be maintained? There were, we must note, four occasions on which the output of the second machine was higher than the average of the first, and an equal number of occasions on which the output of the first machine was lower than the average of the second.

The average over the 15 days for each machine (found by adding the daily outputs and dividing by 15) is 106 for machine A and 97 for machine B. But could the difference between the output of the two machines have occurred by chance in the same way that five heads in succession may occur by chance in the throwing of an unbiased coin, or is there sufficient evidence to justify the belief that there is a real difference in the behaviour of the two machines?

The methods of mathematical statistics enable us to calculate the probability of obtaining by chance this observed difference in machine behaviour if in fact there were no difference between the machines. This is clearly an important tool in O.R. because, as in all scientific and experimental work, it is necessary to distinguish between real and chance effects in order to make satisfactory progress.

Table 2.5.   Output of two machines

Day No.	Machine A	Machine B
1	107	94
2	94	111
3	122	94
4	100	96
5	107	92
6	106	80
7	115	109
8	91	89
9	112	85
10	120	114
11	106	97
12	90	94
13	116	96
14	102	98
15	118	93
16	94	113
Average	118.8	104.3

In the above example the probability that the observed difference between the two machines could have occurred by chance has been calculated and was in fact only 1 in 25; therefore it would have been reasonable to assume that there was a real difference between the two machines. If a much smaller probability were required because, say, it was very important to establish the reality of the difference, then it could be predicted that, if 11 more trials were carried out on each machine and if the same difference in performance persisted, the probability that this difference was still due to chance would have fallen to 1 in 1000.

Note that statistical methods are in this case aiding the planning of experiments so that the best use is made of whatever data are collected.

Discrete Distributions

The normal distribution is continuous in the sense that the variable can take any value between plus and minus infinity. Distributions for which only certain defined values or ranges of values are possible are called discrete. The two most frequently used discrete distributions are the binomial and poisson.

(a) Binomial Distribution

Consider a batch of N items some of which may be defective. In counting the number of defectives in a batch of product, it is not the fact that, say, the

1st, 2nd, and 99th items are defective but that there are 3 items defective which is of interest. In other words, the ability is required to calculate the probability that the batch will contain any specified number of defectives.

From historical data or otherwise, it is possible to say that the chance of any individual item being defective is p. Since an item can only be either defective or non-defective, the chance that an item is non-defective is $(1-p)$. Also, assume that the chance that any item is defective is independent of whether any other item is defective.

Then the chance that the batch of N items contains any particular arrangement of m defectives is $p^m (1-p)^{N-m}$. However, there are many different sequences in which the m defectives could have occurred. To obtain the probability of m defectives, the probability above must be summed over all such possible combinations (sequences). This leads us into 'permutations and combinations', but we will just state the result that the number of ways of arranging m in a series N $(m < N)$ is:

$$\frac{N!}{m!(N-m)!}$$

where the symbol ! means 'factorial', so that

$$N! = N \times (N-1) \times (N-2) \times ... \times 2 \times 1$$

Therefore the chance of getting m defectives in N is $P(m)$, where:

$$P(m) = \frac{N!}{m!(N-m)!} p^m(1-p)^{N-m}$$

This distribution is known as the Binomial Distribution. It can be shown that:

$$\text{Mean} = Np$$
$$\text{Variance} = Np(1-p)$$

The properties of the distribution are completely tabulated and can be found in most statistical tables.

(b) Poisson Distribution

An extension of the Binomial Distribution is that in which N is very large and p very small and yet the average Np is still of reasonable size.

This is the case where there are large numbers of observations each of which is very unlikely to result in the outcome of interest and yet the average is still of reasonable size. Examples are telephone subscribers requiring trunk lines. The chance that any one subscriber will require a trunk line in a given period (one minute say) is very small. Yet there are a large number of subscribers to any exchange, so the average number of trunk calls requested may be sizeable (5, 10, or 100 say). A similar situation is road accidents. The chance that any one individual will have an accident on any one day is extremely small. Yet because of the large number of road users the daily average is high.

It can be shown that the general formula for this distribution is:

$$P(m) = \frac{a^m e^{-a}}{m!}$$

where m is the number of defectives in a large sample N having average α and variance α both equal to $\alpha(N_p)$. Again it is extensively tabulated.

Curve Fitting

Curve fitting is also a technique often used in Operational Research and it will thus be briefly described.

Relationships between two variables are not always unique in the sense that, apart from experimental error, a particular value of one variable necessarily exactly corresponds to the same value of the other variable. An example would be the relationship between the numbers of years spent in receiving education and the salaries for a given age group. If these two variables are plotted for a sample of the population, the result might look like Fig. 2.6.

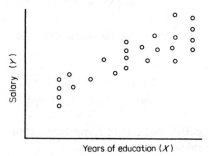

Fig. 2.6.

Graphical representations, of which Fig. 2.6 is an example, are called scatter diagrams. Note that for any particular number of years there is a range of salaries, and vice versa. Most of this variation represents a real variability from person to person in the population, and is dependent on many factors such as home environment, aspects of personality such as drive and ambition, chance experiences, and so on. There is no unique relationship between the variables, but the average salary for a given number of years does tend to increase as years increase.

It may be useful to approximate this relationship with a linear equation:

$$Y = a + bX \qquad (1)$$

There are a number of alternative approaches to estimating the constants a and b from the sample data. The one usually adopted is called the Method of Least Squares. In this approach values for the constants a and b defining the straight line are found which minimize the sum of the square of the deviations of the observed salaries from this line, measured parallel to the salary axis.

It turns out, if one performs the mathematical analysis, that:

(a) The 'best' line passes through the 'centre of gravity' of the n points (x_1, y_1) etc., that is through the point:

$$\bar{x} = \frac{\Sigma x}{n}, \qquad \bar{y} = \frac{\Sigma y}{n} \qquad (2)$$

(b) The 'best' slope of the line is given by:

$$b = \frac{\Sigma (x - \bar{x})(y - \bar{y})}{\Sigma (x - \bar{x})^2} \qquad (3)$$

and the equation of the line becomes:

$$(Y - \bar{y}) = b(X - \bar{x}) \qquad (4)$$

(c) The standard error α of an estimate of y (say y_k) obtained by substituting a value $x = x_k$ in Equation (4) is given by:

$$\alpha = s \sqrt{\left[\frac{1}{n} + \frac{(x_k - \bar{x})^2}{\Sigma(x - \bar{x})^2} \right]} \qquad (5)$$

where

$$s^2 = \frac{\Sigma(y - \bar{y})^2 - b^2 \Sigma(x - \bar{x})^2}{(n - 2)} \qquad (6)$$

Note that, from Equation (5), α is a minimum for $x_k = \bar{x}$. Thus a plot of the 'best' fitting line and the $+\alpha$ and $-\alpha$ limits could look as shown in Fig. 2.7.

Correlation Coefficient

The degree of correlation between n pairs of values of variables x and y is

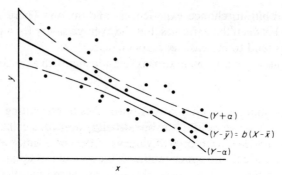

Fig. 2.7. Plot of 'best' fitting line.

usually measured by the correlation coefficient, r, defined by:

$$r = \frac{\text{Covariance of } x \text{ and } y}{\sqrt{[\text{Var}(x) \times \text{Var}(y)]}} \tag{7}$$

or as shown in Equation (8).

$$r = \frac{1}{n} \times \frac{\Sigma(x-\bar{x})(y-\bar{y})}{\sigma_x \sigma_y} \tag{8}$$

where σ_x and σ_y, the standard deviations of x and y, are estimated from the sample of n values.

The coefficient r can lie between $+1$ and -1. A value of $r = +1$ would imply a perfect linear relationship of positive slope between x and y, while $r = -1$ would also imply a perfect linear relationship, but having negative slope.

Other values of r can be roughly interpreted as:

0.0–0.2   virtually no relationship between x and y
0.2–0.4   a 'low' relationship
0.4–0.6   a 'moderate' relationship
0.6–0.8   a 'significant' relationship
0.8–0.1   a 'high' degree of association.

As an example let us determine the best-fit line through the following pairs of values:

x	y
50	2·0
63	2·4
45	1·8
70	2·8
73	2·9
57	2.2

Instead of using Equations (2), (3), and (4) we shall use the equivalent formulae:

$$a = \frac{n\Sigma xy - \Sigma x \Sigma y}{n\Sigma x^2 - (\Sigma x)^2}, \quad b = \frac{\Sigma y - a\Sigma x}{n} \tag{9}$$

since they are easier to use in manual calculations.

x	y	xy	x^2
50	2.0	100	2500
63	2.4	151.2	3969
45	1.8	81	2025
70	2.8	196	4900
73	2.9	211.7	5329
57	2.2	125.4	3249
$\Sigma x = 358$	$\Sigma y = 14.1$	$\Sigma xy = 865.3$	$\Sigma x^2 = 21\,972$

In the example $n = 6$, $(\Sigma x)^2 = 128\,164$. Hence:

$$a = \frac{(6 \times 865.3) - (358 \times 14.1)}{(6 \times 21\,972) - (358 \times 358)} = 0.039$$

$$b = \frac{14.1 - (0.039 \times 358)}{6} = 0.023$$

Thus the equation of the best-fit line is:

$$y = ax + b = 0.039x + 0.023$$

The best-fit line was assumed to be that which minimizes the sum of the squares of the deviations of the original (x, y) values from the line, measured parallel to the y-axis. The deviations and the best-fit line are shown in Fig. 2.8.

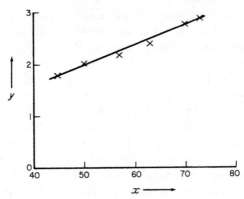

Fig. 2.8.

In this example there is clearly a high degree of correlation between x and y, as demonstrated by Fig. 2.8.

However, this correlation must not be assumed to be due to some process-based relationship between x and y, although this possibility can become a hypothesis for further investigation. An example of this is the correlation found by statisticians between the incidence of lung cancer and tobacco smoking. When first noted, it would have been wrong to assume a cause-and-effect relationship. An alternative proposition, for example, could be that the type of person (emotionally, genetically, etc.) who needs to smoke is also the type of person likely to develop the disease. Since the original analysis was undertaken in the early 1960s, underlying processes connecting lung cancer to chemicals in the tobacco smoke have been found. Thus the statistical analysis established the need to search for the process.

Multiple regression

So far we have discussed the relationship of a variable y to a single variable x. The more general problem occurs when y depends, at least in part, on the values of several other variables, $x_1, ..., x_p$. In this case the relationship can be written:

$$y = b_0 + b_1 x_1 + b_2 x_2 + ... + b_p x_p \qquad (10)$$

The method of least squares can again be applied to the fitting of the above relationship, provided that a 'bank' of data exists. A set of $(p + 1)$ simultaneous equations is established from which the $(p + 1)$ constants, $b_0, b_1, ...,$ b_p, can be determined.

Summary

It has not been the intention in this Chapter to produce a miniature text-book of statistics. This would be impossible. Some of the concepts and ideas of mathematical statistics have therefore merely been introduced, and many important concepts, such as the Central Limit Theorem, have not been discussed. The purpose of this Chapter was really to show that there is an armoury of statistical methods to enable the maximum information to be extracted from numerical data. Further information can be obtained from the books listed at the end of this Chapter.

Statistical techniques serve three purposes in Operational Research. One is to enable real results to be distinguished from chance ones, another is to assist in the planning of investigations so that the maximum use is made of the results, and the third is to enable predictions to be made about the frequency with which certain numbers will occur by chance in particular situations. More will be said about this third use of statistical methods in the chapter on Stock and Production Control Models (Chapter 6).

BIBLIOGRAPHY

Buitson, A. and Keen, J., *Essentials of Quality Control*, Heinemann, 1965.

Davies O.L. (Ed.), *Statistical Methods in Research and Production*, 2nd Ed., Oliver and Boyd, 1949.

Davies O.L. (Ed.), *Design and Analysis of Industrial Experiments*, Oliver and Boyd, 1963.

Feigenbaum, A.V., *Quality Control: Principles, Practice and Administration*, McGraw-Hill.

Moroney, M.J., *Facts from Figures*, Penguin Books, 1951.

Paradine, C.G. and Rivett, B.H.P., *Statistical Methods for Technologists*, 2nd Ed., English Universities Press, 1964.

Phillips, L.D., *Bayesian Statistics for Social Scientists*, Nelson, 1973.

Reichmann, W.J., *Use and Abuse of Statistics*, Methuen, 1962.

Topping, J., *Errors of Observation and Their Treatment*, Institute of Physics Monograph, 1955.

Weatherburn, C.E., *Mathematical Statistics*, Cambridge University Press, 1952.

Mendenhall, W. and Reinmuth, J.E., *Statistics for Management and Economics*, Wadsworth (1974).

Wonnacott, T.H. and Wonnacott, R.J., *Introductory Statistics for Business and Economics*, Wiley (1972).

Daniel, W.W. and Terrell, J.C., *Business Statistics Basic Concepts and Methodology*, Houghton Mifflin (1975).

3 Queuing Problems

Ah, 'All things come to those who wait,'
(I say these words to make me glad),
But something answers, soft and sad,
'They come, but often come too late'.

Mary Montgomerie Singleton; Tout Vient à Qui Sait Attendre

Having learnt how to measure uncertainty we can now put it to good effect by using our knowledge in one of the most difficult of administrative situations – dealing with queues. This chapter follows logically from the first part of Chapter 2; perhaps this will set at ease any otherwise conscientious busy manager who has only had time to read that.

We are all familiar with queues and have to join a queue from time to time. If too many people arrive at a shop in a given time a queue forms; if too many aircraft arrive for landing permission at an airport they have to be 'stacked'; most of us have queued for petrol at some time. Most factories are operated on the principle of having queues so that work can be continually fed into a department without the periods of idle time which might ensue if there were no queues. In this case a queue may be a good thing, helping to assist in economic planning of the department's work. If the queue becomes too large, however, difficulties arise. The pace of work may be stepped up to reduce the queue, and, unless the increased pace is within the capacity of the department, efficiency may fall, leading to the queue being lengthened rather than shortened.

Priorities may be resorted to, and this can be very dangerous because the transfer of jobs to a higher place in the queue only results in lengthening the average waiting time of all remaining jobs, which may increase the need for further priorities, and so a cycle of panic measures sets in.

For service-giving departments, such as millwrights, a queue of work can be a very inefficient thing to have. If too many machines need repair at the same time the consequences can be serious. Similarly, a queue of ships waiting to be unloaded at a port can be very costly, and a series of wharves waiting for ships is an expensive way of using capital. The problem of queues and how they should be serviced is a major problem for many organizations.

A mathematical theory of queues has been developed which enables O.R.

workers to calculate for a given situation what kind of queue will result and how long the items will have to wait before service. For some common problems, certain conclusions of this theory are sufficiently concise to be worth stating here.

In the first place, the probability of having a queue varies more or less directly with the proportion of time that the service provided is going to be in demand. Thus, if a service is used to 80% of its capacity, the probability that there will be a queue is about 8 out of 10, i.e. in 8 out of 10 calls on that service we shall have to wait before being served. (Although this is strictly true only for a queuing system with a single server, for random arrivals, and for a distribution of service times known as negative exponential, it is approximately true for most common systems.)

This is something that we all observe in practice. If we frequently visit a shop with several assistants and are always served immediately, we notice that some of the assistants have no customers to see to. If on the other hand we call at a busy newsagent's every morning and there is only one man serving behind the counter, we almost invariably have to wait a while.

The meaning of this relationship between service capacity and queue probability is that if we carefully plan a service department so that it has just enough capacity to meet expected demand then we can expect a queue to exist at all times and to grow continually.

If at the other extreme we want to meet every demand almost immediately, we must expect the department to spend about half its time in idleness. This explains the perpetual headache of anyone in charge of such a department – how to arrange things so that a reasonable service is provided and yet the work force is fully occupied. In this situation the man who keeps the odd painting job up his sleeve is not really making work for his men, he is ensuring that his department can give a good service and yet not appear to be over-staffed.

The relationship between queuing and service rates can be illustrated diagrammatically using cost curves as shown in Fig. 3.1. At slow service rates, queues build up and the cost of queuing increases. If we increase the service rate this costs money, but the cost of queuing goes down. We really need to find the minimum cost of operating the complete system.

The other main conclusion which emerges from the theory of queues is that the more haphazard the arrivals the greater is the customer's expected waiting time. This is because with haphazard arrivals a time may come when no demands on the server are made for a long period. That time is lost from the system and when subsequently a bunch of arrivals occurs it takes a long time for the system to catch up and disperse the resulting backlog.

To ensure that reasonably rapid service can be provided it is advisable to arrange that the service-giving department – or production unit – is not loaded to its full capacity but to, on average, about say 80% of its capacity

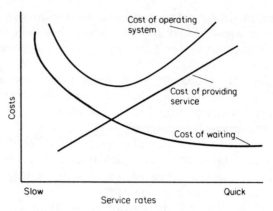

Fig. 3.1. Costs of queuing system.

and that the demands on it are made as uniformly as possible.

This is common sense, of course, and most managers do not need an Operational Research study to know this. There are many situations, however, in which they may wish to know precisely how long items may have to wait in a queue for a given service capacity so that they can decide whether to provide extra capacity, at extra cost, or let the items wait a little longer and risk the losses which may arise from giving a less satisfactory service.

Here again the O.R. worker can set up a mathematical model of the system and study its properties and so learn something of the likely behaviour of the system in real life.

Problem solutions

For solving queuing problems mathematically an expression known as the traffic intensity is used. This is the demand divided by the capacity, or more precisely the mean service time divided by the mean interval between successive arrivals. It is usually given the Greek symbol ρ. The calculation of the traffic intensity for any system is relatively simple. The time intervals between the arrivals of jobs or customers or whatever it is that is being served are measured and the average of these intervals is determined. A good method of making sure that an accurate measure of the average has been obtained, and not one that has been influenced unduly by one or two unusually long or short intervals, is to plot the cumulative average against the number of arrivals as in the following example.

Suppose the arrival intervals, to the nearest minute, were:

5, 4, 10, 6, 3, 2, 6, 4, 8, 15, 2, 5, 4, 6, 8, 7, 3,

5, 2, 6, 8, 7, 4, 3, 2, 6, 7, 5, 3, 4, 6, 5, 8, 4

The cumulative totals, obtained by adding the first two intervals and then the first three and so on, are:

9, 19, 25, 28, 30, 36, 40, 48, 63, 65, 70, 74, 80, 88, 95, 98, 103, 105, 111, 119, 126, 130, 133, 135, 141, 148, 153, 156, 160, 166, 171, 179, 183

The cumulative averages obtained by dividing all the cumulative totals by the number of intervals making up each total are as follows:

$$9/_2, 19/_3, 25/_4, 28/_5, ..., 183/_{34}$$

or in decimal notation:

$$4.5, 6.3, 6.2, 5.6, ..., 5.4$$

When these cumulative averages are plotted against the number of intervals the result is that shown in Fig. 3.2. It fluctuates a little at first but then settles

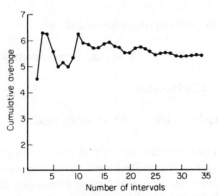

Fig. 3.2. Cumulative average plotted against number of intervals.

down to a fairly steady value of 5.4 minutes. This is the value to take as the average interval between arrivals.

The average service time can be found in a similar way. For example, it may be 4.5 minutes; in this instance the traffic intensity would be:

$$\rho = 4.5/5.4 = 0.833$$

It has been shown that in simple queuing systems where there is only one service point and hence only one queue, as in the case of a tobacconist's counter or of a single man working a machine in a millwright's shop, the following relationships are true.

The customer's average waiting time (including the time being served), again measured over a fairly long period, is:

$$\frac{1}{1 - \rho} \times \text{ mean service time}$$

The probability of not having to queue is $(1 - \rho)$, and hence the percentage of time the server is utilized is $(\rho \times 100)$.

These apply strictly only in cases where both the arrival intervals and service times vary at random with a particular kind of distribution. But this distribution is common in queuing situations, and so that relationships can be used in many cases.

Thus, in the example that we have worked out, the mean waiting time would be:

$$\frac{1}{1 - 0.833} \times 4.5 = 27 \text{ minutes}$$

the probability of not having to queue would be:

$$1 - 0.833 = 0.167, \text{ i.e. approximately } 17\%$$

and the server would be busy for:

$$0.833 \times 100 = 83.3\% \text{ of its time}$$

These figures might be tolerable, but if the demand increases so that the mean arrival interval becomes 5 minutes, then the mean waiting time increases sharply to 45 minutes. In fact, with traffic intensities above 0.8 the mean waiting time rapidly increases with any increase in traffic intensity, as shown in Fig. 3.3.

This shows how bottlenecks can arise when there is a slight increase in demand in systems where traffic intensity is high. It should be remembered

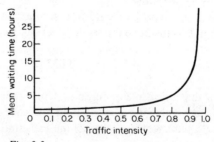

Fig. 3.3.

that we have been working out average times and have not looked at the rate of build-up of a queue or its shortening by increased service. Congestion may sometimes be very slow to build up, as shown in Fig. 3.4 which is reproduced from a paper by Robinson. The traffic intensity was 0.96 and it was not until 250 arrivals had been dealt with that the waiting time became excessive in this particular simulation study.

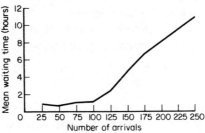

Fig. 3.4. Increase in mean waiting time with time.

Equally, however, the congestion may be very slow to disperse unless the traffic intensity is reduced very considerably below 1.0 by excessive overtime working or by employing extra services or machines. It is therefore wise not to allow the traffic intensity at any servicing point to approach unity unless means are available for reducing it very considerably if necessary. The likely bottlenecks in any complex system can be estimated by computing the traffic intensities at each service point and noting that those in excess of 0.8 are likely to cause trouble.

We have worked out average values of waiting times, but these conceal the fact that actual waiting times vary considerably. If the situation is not stable and the rates of arrival and service are changing, analysis of the problem using our queuing theory methods may be misleading. We would probably use simulation methods, discussed in Chapter 5, in such cases.

In the paper by Robinson, already referred to, an estimating section of a Production Engineering Department found itself occasionally unable to meet requests at short notice owing to severe short-term fluctuations, even though its traffic intensity was usually only about 0.72. This problem was solved by having a third estimator on call to deal with emergencies. His presence lowered the traffic intensity to 0.48 and enabled a very rapid service to be provided when necessary. He was, of course, employed on other work when not required for estimating.

Economics of Queuing

This last example leads to the problem of deciding on the best service to provide. How do we define 'best'? In most situations it is a question of economics, and the balancing of two conflicting costs, as in Fig. 3.1.

As a simple illustration let us return to our previous example, and assume that a study has been made of the cost of waiting and providing service. The cost of providing service at an average service time of 4.5 minutes is £12 per hour, and the cost of waiting is £3 per hour per person queuing. For the present system the total cost of operating per hour becomes:

$$\text{Total cost} = \text{serving cost} + \text{queuing cost}$$
$$= £12 + 3 \times \text{(number of arrivals in 1 hour)} \times \text{(average waiting time in hours)}$$
$$= £12 + 3 \times \frac{60}{5.4} \times \frac{27}{60} = £27$$

The service time may be altered with an accompanying change in cost. In this case let the cost be inversely proportional to the service time s, i.e.

Cost of providing service at an average serving time of s minutes

$$\text{per customer} = \frac{£12 \times 4.5}{s} = \frac{£54}{s}$$

We can now put the two costs together and the total cost can be recalculated for various values of the average service time. For our example the results are shown in Fig. 3.5 and Table 3.1, from where it is seen that the most economic way of operating the system overall would be to have an average service time of 3.5 minutes. In many cases the possible service time changes in discrete amounts when an extra server is added, and in such cases we have only a few alternatives to consider, rather than a continuous choice.

The problem of estimating the cost of queuing is probably the most difficult task for the manager, rather than doing the calculations. A case quoted by Churchman is a famous illustration of this point. The manager of a large hotel was receiving complaints about the time people were having to wait for the lift. Certain possible unfavourable solutions such as putting in

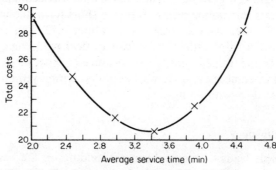

Fig. 3.5. Total costs as a function of service time.

Table 3.1.   Queuing costs.

Av. service time (min)	Cost of service	Cost of waiting	Total cost
2.0	27.0	1.76	28.76
2.5	21.60	2.59	24.19
3.0	18.00	3.75	21.75
3.4	15.88	5.10	20.98
3.5	15.43	5.52	20.95
3.6	15.00	6.00	21.00
4.0	13.50	8.57	22.07
4.5	12.00	15.00	27.00
5.0	10.80	37.50	48.30

a new lift (at great cost) came to mind. Luckily he brought in an O.R. student to help him and he solved the problem at negligible cost. You will have to read the original reference to get the whole story, but the main solution was to install mirrors by the lift sides. The ladies looked in the mirrors and forgot about complaining, and the men were too busy looking at the ladies to complain. Many morals can be drawn from this, one of them being that it is often very difficult to measure the cost of certain activities.

By employing the mathematics of queuing theory, a manager is able quickly to assess the probable efficiency of a system in terms of its service-provision or productive capacity, to estimate the likely bottlenecks and plan to eliminate them. If queues are inevitable, or desirable on economic terms, the manager needs to calculate their likely lengths and their possible variation. In this problem, queuing problems are linked with stock and production control problems considered in Chapter 6.

We have only been able to illustrate the nature of queues and queuing theory. Anyone interested in pursuing the subject further may wish to consult the books by Lee or Page, but you should be warned that the use of mathematics is unavoidable. Many complex queuing problems can be tackled but the mathematics becomes so difficult that simulation techniques (Chapter 5) are required.

REFERENCES

Churchman, C.W., Ackoff, R.L. and Arnoff, E.L., *Introduction to Operations Research*, Wiley, 1957.
Lee, A.M., *Applied Queuing Theory*, Macmillan, London, 1966.
Page, E., *Queuing Theory in O.R.*, Butterworths, London, 1972.
Robinson, F.D. and Duckworth, W.E., *An Application of Queuing Theory to the Speed of Estimating*, First International Conference on Operation Research, English Universities Press, 1957.

4 Business Forecasting

'Cheshire-Puss,' she began, rather timidly ....
'Would you tell me please, which way I ought to go from here?'
'That depends a good deal on where you want to get to,' said the Cat.
'I don't much care where,' said Alice.
'Then it doesn't matter which way you go,' said the Cat.

Lewis Carroll

The making of forecasts is an essential aspect of our life, whether we are concerned with forecasts of the weather, of sales demand for a product, or of the power needs of the nation. Estimates are needed because decisions of many types will depend on the forecast values of the variables. Examples of areas where forecasting can play an important role in decision-taking occur in sales prediction, manpower planning, acquisition of plant, market planning, publicity campaigning, research and development planning, local government planning for various services, national planning of the economy, stocking policy in warehouses, purchasing policy, and production control.

As illustrated in Chapter 1 forecasting plays such an important, if often unsuspected part, in the life of any Company, that it must be an integral part of an operational research function.

Forecasting is made difficult where important uncontrollable forces act outside the organization in which the forecaster operates. Examples are external competition, national and local economic factors, political environment, technological developments, and social behaviour.

If relevant forecasts are to be made, the organization needs to be coordinated across functional areas. For example, marketing planners must be aware of the possible influence of a new product development programme in the research and development department.

Before considering techniques of forecasting it is appropriate to identify three distinct categories of forecast:

Short term – one week or one month ahead; necessary for the daily planning and allocation of existing resources.

Medium term – one to five years ahead; required as basic information for annual budgeting, corporate planning, and to affect marketing plans and business policy.

Long term – five to fifteen years ahead; necessary for developing plans for the long-term survival and success of the organization.

The forecasts themselves may take one of several forms. A single figure for the probability of penetrating a particular market segment up to a given percentage level constitutes a forecast, as does a subjectively based opinion about the future movement of world copper prices. In the rest of this section we categorize techniques of forecasting from the more subjective to the more objective. You will note that the techniques also tend to fall into one of two categories: exploratory or normative. Exploratory methods are based on an extrapolation of historical data, and tend to neglect internal or external changes. On the other hand, normative methods, which tend to be applied more to medium-term and long-term forecasting, work backwards from a possible future state to the present time. Once a possible future is defined in socio-economic terms, the organization can plan to meet that future, if it so desires. In practice one or more techniques may be used in combination, or some approach which is special to the situation devised. For brevity we have categorized the techniques into: intuitive thinking; trend extrapolation; morphological analysis; relevance analysis; dynamic modelling.

Intuitive thinking

Intuitive forecasting is based on informal thinking about the future without recourse to external data or analysis in a very formalized manner. The forecast may be produced by an individual or by a group, and so a number of approaches can be identified.

Individual thinking

An expert produces a forecast without interaction with others. The problem with a forecast of this kind is that the thought processes are unlikely to be made explicit; they thus pass unquestioned, and the quality of the output depends on the accumulated knowledge and experience of an individual.

Opinion polls

A group of experts individually produce a forecast and the results are then pooled in some way to arrive at an 'average' judgement. No interaction takes place between the experts.

Brainstorming

A panel of experts is brought together to produce a forecast after interaction and discussion. A shortcoming of this approach is that the more persuasive and/or dominant personalities may force their opinions on the group.

Delphi analysis

This approach was developed in order to reduce the shortcomings of individual thinking, opinion polls, and brainstorming. A group of 'experts' are each asked, by means of a carefully designed questionnaire, to predict the timing and effect of future events. Without face-to-face contact, the experts are then provided with feedback regarding differences and agreements among the replies. A second questionnaire may then be completed individually as before and the process repeated until a stable set of opinions is (hopefully) established or a consensus achieved.

Much of science fiction consists of this type of intuitive forecasting and still enjoys a considerable public reputation for very-long-range forecasting. However, while it was possible for imaginative writers in the 19th century and the first decades of the 20th century to catch up somehow with broad scientific progress and to place their stories on a reasonable basis which did not conflict very seriously with natural laws and technical non-impossibilities, these elements of 'serious' science fiction have become less and less accessible to writers who are not professionals in science or technology. There is no Jules Verne in our day, nor is there a science fiction writer who could portray character so well.

A brilliant critique of 20th century science fiction has been made by Gabor, pointing out the basic trend of sentimental out-of-this-world optimism prevailing in the West up to 1930, and still in full flourish in Russia today (where it even penetrates into supposedly serious forecasts). As a source for the recognition of social goals and of mankind's great aspirations, this type of science fiction is of minor value only. Nor does the dreary 'space opera' genre which abounds today contribute anything in this direction.

Intuitive thinking may be placed on a slightly better footing through the development of a certain sophistication in the selection of experts, and possibly, as Gordon and Helmer suggest, by using schemes for a self-appraisal of competence, corrections by feedback procedures, etc.

An interesting approach to the improvement of intuitive expert forecasts and the reduction of the 'noise level' implicit in intuitive forecasting has been developed by Abt Associates and made part of their comprehensive operational models, including models for technological forecasting. In this approach, incremental forecasting of short-term changes by experts is iterated by applying the appropriate quantitative corrective bias to the next round of predictions (see Fig. 4.1). "In this way, the expert predictions will gradually approach a stable path, which will not normally be absolutely

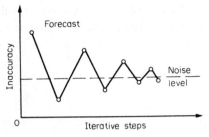

Fig. 4.1.

accurate, but which will be inaccurate to a constant degree. This level of inaccuracy can be defined as the 'noise level' for any particular predicted change. Within the range thus defined, there will be no bias for preferring one prediction over another, but outside the range (which may well become narrower as time goes on, compensating for increasing possibilities) predictions can usefully be compared and evaluated".

Thomas and McCrory of the Battelle Memorial Institute developed a method for synthesizing expert opinion and testing the sensitivity to deviation by an individual expert; this method has not yet been published.

Helmer remarks that there are two kinds of experts, generalists and specialists, and that both kinds should be used for intuitive forecasts. The ways in which experts can be deployed are classified by Helmer into a symmetric pattern (several experts on the same problem) and an asymmetric pattern (different experts on different aspects of a problem). The development of a rationale for the use of experts is one of the important tasks in the area of social technology.

In studying supposedly intuitive forecasts of future technologies, one finds in general that they represent rather cluttered pieces of systematic thinking, uncritical extrapolations of the present state-of-the-art, and recapitulations of other forecasts. The 'World in 1984' series in *New Scientist*, which elicited contributions from many of the leading minds in a wide variety of technological areas, demonstrates the limited usefulness of intuitive thinking for exploratory purposes; the substantial contributions reflected a more systematic attitude, or an approach from the normative side.

For very-long-range exploratory forecasting, meaning time-frames of 50 years and more, intuitive thinking is, of course, less limited than systematic thinking. On the other hand, at that range it may be nearly tantamount to a 'serious' version of science fiction (respecting laws of nature etc.).

Trend Extrapolation

A parameter that is capable of clear definition is plotted against time from historical data in order to extrapolate and predict future values. The extrapolation can be done by hand or by mathematical curve fitting. The assumption is that the factors causing the historical shape of the curve will continue to operate in the future. We will now consider a series of extrapolation methods.

Curve fitting

The historical data may appear to fit one of a number of mathematical functions. The most common of these are:
(1) Linear change:

$$y = a + bt$$

where *a* and *b* are constants, *y* is the value of the variable of interest, and *t* represents time. The speed of aircraft, as shown in Fig. 4.2, is an example of this type of function. The constants *a* and *b* represent respectively the vertical intercept and the slope of the line.

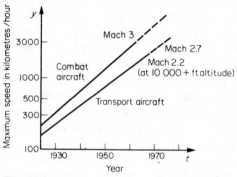

Fig. 4.2.

(2) Linear change with 'flattening' as a limit is approached (Fig. 4.3). The limit may be imposed by physical or legal laws. The efficiency of thermal power plants exhibits these characteristics for example, and also the mechanization of human work (expressed in terms of the decrease in annual working hours per man).

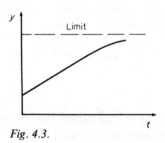

Fig. 4.3.

(3) Parabolic rate of change:

$$y = a + bt + ct^2$$

where a, b, and c are constants. An example is the operating energy of particle accelerators as shown in Fig. 4.4.

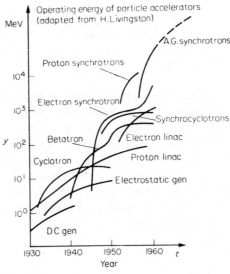

Fig. 4.4.

(4) Exponential growth:

$$y = ae^{bt}$$

where a and b are constants. A good example is the almost precisely exponential increase in energy conversion efficiency (lumens per watt) in illumination technology from the paraffin candle to the gallium arsenide diode.

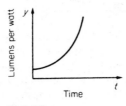

Fig. 4.5.

(5) An S-shaped growth curve (Fig. 4.6). The early part of this curve is sometimes difficult to distinguish from exponential growth. S-shaped curves

are the normal characteristic of specific maturing technologies. A good example is the proportion of Gross National Product spent on R & D in the years 1900–1970 in the U.K. and U.S.A.

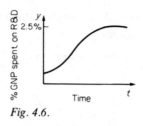

Fig. 4.6.

   Exponential growth has been a characteristic of many world parameters and has been causing alarm in many places. Examples of this growth are shown in Figs. 4.7 and 4.8. Ultimately these curves must become S-shaped if the world, as we know it, is to survive. Many hitherto exponentially growing technologies have finally settled down to S-shaped growth as shown in Fig. 4.9. The data for each of these possible relationships can be analysed by the methods described in Chapter 2 (see page 26), so that the values of the constants are objectively determined. This has the advantage of allowing an estimate of the standard deviation of the forecast and hence a confidence interval to be determined.

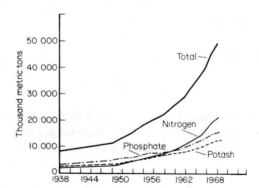

Fig. 4.7. World fertilizer consumption (excluding U.S.S.R. and People's Republic of China). The consumption is increasing exponentially, with a doubling time of about 10 years. Total use is now five times greater than it was during World War II. [From U.N. Department of Economic and Social Affairs, *Statistical Yearbook 1955, 1960,* and *1970,* United Nations, New York, 1956, 1961, and 1971.]

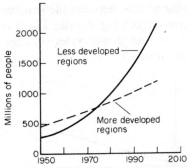

Fig. 4.8. World urban population. Total urban population is expected to increase exponentially in the less well developed regions of the world, but almost linearly in the more developed regions. Present average doubling time for city populations in less developed regions is 15 years. [From U.N. Department of Economic and Social Affairs, *The World Population Situation in 1970*, United Nations, New York, 1971.]

The horizontal axis may not always be time. For example this approach may be used where the development of one technological capability or other parameter is known to precede the development of another owing to social, economic, or technical linkages. A commonly quoted example for this is

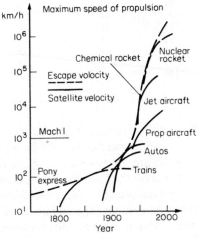

Fig. 4.9.

the steadily increasing lag in time between the maximum speed of military and civilian aircraft derived from Fig. 4.2 (see Fig. 4.10). Another example could be a relationship between annual sales volumes and total consumer expenditure on pharmaceuticals.

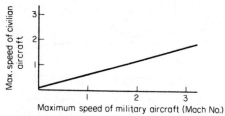

Fig. 4.10.

Moving averages

A commonly used and simple method of forecasting involves the calculation and projection of a moving average. This method 'smooths out' random fluctuations in the data. For example, consider the sales information in Table 4.1.

Table 4.1.   Time series of annual sales in 1000's.

(1) Time period	(2) No. of sales	(3) 3-period moving average (rounded to interest values)	(4) Trend difference from last moving average (rounded)
1	81		
2	91	87	
3	90	89	+2
4	85	91	+2
5	97	94	+3
6	101	99	+5
7	99	102	+3
8	105		
9			

Columns (1) and (2) contain the basic historical information regarding the number of units, e.g. washing machines, sold by a retail outlet in each of eight prior years. For stocking purposes a prediction for the coming year (year 9) is required. In column (3) the rounded averages of the sales numbers are calculated in threes. For example, $(81 + 91 + 90)/3 = 87^{1}/_{3}$ which rounds to 87 as shown in the table. In column (4) trend differences are obtained by calculating the difference between a given moving average in column (3) and its predecessor. Thus $2 = (89 - 87)$, and so on. Some of the differences could, of course, be negative. Taking averages in threes has in this case caused all the differences to be positive. The forecast for period 9 can be obtained by taking the last moving average (102 for period 7), and adding twice the value of the latest trend difference, $2 \times (+3) = 6$, giving a prediction for period 9 of 108 machines.

In this example the data were averaged in threes, depending on the amount of relevant historical data and the degree of fluctuation. Moving averages can be taken in fours or fives, etc. More generally, there may be a trend, seasonal variation, and random fluctuation present in the data. An example of the extension of moving averages to take account of seasonal variations is given by Battersby who points out that seasonal effects usually follow an annual rhythm, because they are generated by one fundamental cause: the inclination of the earth's axis to the plane of its orbit. The effects of this occur in various ways, some being shown in Table 4.2.

Table 4.2.   Seasonal effects on sales.

Prime cause	Secondary cause	Examples of goods affected
Variations in sunlight	Intensity of sunlight	Sunglasses, camera films, sun-tan lotions
	Length of day	Lamp bulbs, premium grade petrol, theatre seats, books
Other aspects of the weather	Temperature	Coal, clothing, soft drinks, anti-freeze, contraceptives
	Rainfall	Raincoats, umbrellas, certain drugs
	Fog	Foglamps, winter cruises
Feasts,	Easter	Chocolate, greetings cards
religious	Christmas/Yule	Turkeys, fir-trees, toys, wines and spirits
historical	Thanksgiving	Turkeys, aspirin
	Guy Fawkes' Day	Fireworks, burn dressings
political or commercial	Independence Day Bank Holidays Father's Day	Travel, resort facilities Tobacco

Seasonal effects are generally measured above and below the average for the year, so their total over a whole year is zero. (Sometimes the average is first adjusted for secular trend, as will be shown later.) It is for this reason that moving totals and averages are so often taken over a time-span of a single year or exact multiples of it.

Weighted moving averages

One of the disadvantages of using the moving averages method is that *equal* weight is given to all the values in calculating the moving averages themselves. In fact, experience of a situation may be that the most recent value(s) of a variable provides the most reliable predictions. One quite commonly used example of this is known as the exponential smoothing method. In this case the latest moving average (M_t) is given in terms of the previous moving average (M_{t-1}) by the relation:

$$M_t = M_{t-1} + a(Y_t - M_{t-1})$$

where t denotes a time period, Y_t is the current observation, and a is a constant weighting factor which takes a value between 0 and 1. The equation is equivalent to the statement: the new forecast = old forecast + $a \times$ (latest observation − old forecast). By rearranging the equation an alternative form is:

$$M_t = aY_t + (1 - a) M_{t-1}$$

Analogously M_{t-1} is given by:

$$M_{t-1} = aY_{t-1} + (1 - a) M_{t-2}$$

and so on for M_{t-2}, M_{t-3}, etc. Substituting M_{t-1}, M_{t-2}, M_{t-3}, etc., back into the original equation leads to the expansion:

$$M_t = aY_t + a(1 - a)\, Y_{t-1} + \ldots + (1 - a)^r\, Y_{t-r} + \ldots$$

This equation shows that previous values of the variable are multiplied by powers of the same value, $(1 - a)$, and this is why this particular calculation is know as an exponentially smoothed average. The form of the equation means that the value for M_t can be easily calculated since it depends only on M_{t-1} and Y_t. If a series of values for the variable is available, this can be used to determine the value of a that minimizes the sum of the squares of the deviations given by:

$$\sum_t (M_t - Y_{t+1})^2$$

This is conveniently done by trial and error: for example, by setting $a = 0.5$, 0.4, 0.3 to see which gives the smallest value of the above summation, so eventually reaching a 'best' value for a by iteration.

Autocorrelation

This approach makes use of the past values of a series in order to predict a future value or values. The central assumption is that the present value of a series is given by a function of its previous values. The function is usually assumed to be linear. The correlation coefficient r_l (see Chapter 2, page 27) for the data at any previous time lag l is calculated from the pairs of values:

$$y_i \text{ and } Y_{i-l}, \text{ for } i = t, t - 1, ..., t - l + 1$$

The value of r_l plotted against l is a function called the autocorrelation function. It is analogous to the correlation coefficient of a pair of variables x and y described on page 27. This function can be studied to see which 'lagged' values should be included in the prediction formula. Data with cyclic variations, perhaps due to seasonal factors, will have a high value of r_l for l about equal to the period of the cycle. The form of the prediction formula is:

$$Y_p = a_0 + X_n a_p + X_{n-1} a_{p+1} + ... + X_i a_{p+n-i} + ... + X_1 a_{p+n-1}$$

where p is the number of periods ahead for which the predicted value, Y_p, is required as shown in Fig. 4.11.

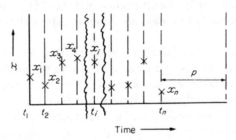

Fig. 4.11.

Most computers have standard multiple linear regression packages making the calculation of a_0 and a_{p+n-i} relatively straightforward once the values for the lags, l, have been decided from the significant values of r_l deduced from the autocorrelation function.

The procedure also allows the standard error of the forecast to be calculated as part of the routine. Box and Jenkins have developed the autocorrelation method further. In essence the autocorrelation function is itself examined in order to see whether there are any significant correlations present in the autocorrelation function in the same way as in the original data. This process is repeated until at some stage no significant correlations remain. It is only worth going to this degree of sophistication for well-behaved time series where no additional factors affect things. A relatively long time series of data is also necessary.

Morphological Analysis

This method was first suggested by Zwicky in order to ensure the identification of all possible solutions to a stated problem. The first step is to define the function to be performed as clearly as possible. This principal function is then analysed into its essential component parts, and all the ways of meeting each component requirement are listed. The complete set of alternative solutions is then generated by combining members of the component subsets.

For example, a transportation system may require a means of propulsion, of changing direction, and of changing speed. In turn, the energy for propulsion might be obtained from chemical fuel, nuclear fuel, solar energy conversion, and so on. Each possible solution to the overall problem, identified in this way, can then be evaluated in technical and economic terms. At this stage it is probable that one or more of the other techniques would also be used in order to produce an actual forecast.

There are, in particular, three types of generic problem which the morphological analysis attempts to solve.

(a) How much information about a certain limited set of phenomena can be obtained with the help of a given class of device? Or, stated differently, what devices are necessary to obtain all the information about a given set of phenomena?

(b) What is the sequence of all effects issuing from a certain cause?

(c) Deduce all the devices of a given class, or all the methods of a given class, or, generally speaking, all the solutions of a given definite problem.

An answer to the second type of question is found in the relevance (or hereditary) tree, which will be discussed in its normative aspects below.

The third type of problem is the crucial one for exploratory forecasting and will be discussed here in greater detail.

The morphological method is simply an orderly way of looking at things and so achieving a systematic perspective over all the possible solutions of a given large-scale problem. It provides a framework for thinking in basic principles and parameters which is growing in importance even if practised in a disordered or *ad hoc* fashion.

An example (Fig. 4.12) may illustrate its practical application. It concerns the totality of all jet engines which are composed of simple elements and activated by chemical energy, reflecting knowledge in 1951.

Zwicky remarks: "This, if no internal contradictions were present, would make possible the following number of pure medium jet engines.

$$2 \times 2 \times 3 \times 2 \times 2 \times 4 \times 4 \times 4 \times 3 \times 2 \times 2 = 36864$$

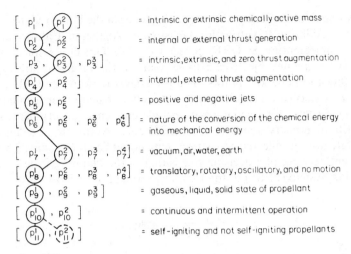

$$[\; p_1^1 \; , \; p_1^2 \;]$$ = intrinsic or extrinsic chemically active mass

$$[\; p_2^1 \; , \; p_2^2 \;]$$ = internal or external thrust generation

$$[\; p_3^1 \; , \; p_3^2 \; , \; p_3^3 \;]$$ = intrinsic, extrinsic, and zero thrust augmentation

$$[\; p_4^1 \; , \; p_4^2 \;]$$ = internal, external thrust augmentation

$$[\; p_5^1 \; , \; p_5^2 \;]$$ = positive and negative jets

$$[\; p_6^1 \; , \; p_6^2 \; , \; p_6^3 \; , \; p_6^4 \;]$$ = nature of the conversion of the chemical energy into mechanical energy

$$[\; p_7^1 \; , \; p_7^2 \; , \; p_7^3 \; , \; p_7^4 \;]$$ = vacuum, air, water, earth

$$[\; p_8^1 \; , \; p_8^2 \; , \; p_8^3 \; , \; p_8^4 \;]$$ = translatory, rotatory, oscillatory, and no motion

$$[\; p_9^1 \; , \; p_9^2 \; , \; p_9^3 \;]$$ = gaseous, liquid, solid state of propellant

$$[\; p_{10}^1 \; , \; p_{10}^2 \;]$$ = continuous and intermittent operation

$$[\; p_{11}^1 \; , \; p_{11}^2 \;]$$ = self-igniting and not self-igniting propellants

Fig. 4.12.

These jet engines would contain single simple elements only and being activated by chemical energy. However, there are some internal restrictions which reduce the above number to 25344 possible simple engines". A first evaluation, in 1943, on the basis of lower parameters, arrived at only 576 possibilities, which, however, correctly included the then secret German pulse-jet powered aerial bomb V-1 and the V-2 rocket.

One may recall, in this context, the fatal failure of Lindemann, Churchill's scientific adviser, to recognize the potential of the V-2 even when he was shown photographs. "It will not fly" is plausibly explained by his exclusive preoccupation with solid propellants, stubbornly rejecting the idea of liquid propellants.

Relevance analysis

The main objective of a complete programme is first defined. From this definition a number of constraints and conditions are listed, from which a set of sub-objectives is defined. The process is then repeated with each sub-objective until levels of detail are reached at which individual contributing projects and tasks are defined. The above analysis can be represented diagrammatically, using a structure known as a relevance tree, if desired. In defining the objectives at each level it is likely that other forecasting techniques will be required.

The concept of relevance trees was first suggested by Churchman and others, in connection with decision-making in general industrial contexts.

Qualitative relevance trees are employed to aid decision-making and are called technology trees. One such tree for semiconductor technology is used by one of the big semiconductor companies in the United States. North American Aviation's Autonetics Division in Anaheim, California, is at present implementing SCORE (Select Concrete Objectives for Research Emphasis) to relate objectives 5 to 15 years in the future to strategy and tactics and to define key points. The three-level relevance tree (Fig. 4.13) chosen is patterned on an electronic company's structure for technological planning. Criteria for selection will include customer (government) needs, competition, industry trends, and the resources of Autonetics. The main aim is to relate distant objectives to action that should be taken today. The most prominent example of a decision tree is that of the Planning-Programming-Budgeting System (PPBS) of the U.S. Department of Defense.

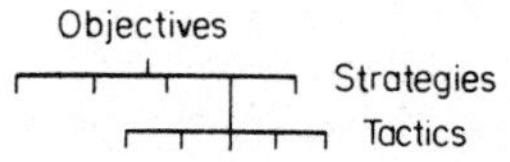

Objectives

Strategies

Tactics

Fig. 4.13.

The first large-scale application of relevance trees to numerical analysis for decision-making has been made by Honeywell's Military and Space Sciences Department in Washington D.C. This is the famous PATTERN (Planning Assistance Through Technical Evaluation of Relevance Numbers) scheme which was first used for Honeywell's aeronautical and space activities in 1963, and was extended in 1964 into a comprehensive scheme covering all military and space activities in which Honeywell is interested directly or indirectly. This scheme, continually being extended and refined, will serve as the best basis for an explanation of PATTERN, which has been described in various publications.

The scheme of tasks to be accomplished before a computer programme can be set up is illustrated in Fig. 4.14.

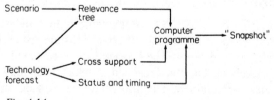

Fig. 4.14.

A qualitative scenario attempts to assess national objectives, activities, missions, etc. in the period between 1970 and 1980, and possibly beyond. These findings are then used for the construction of the relevance tree and the assignment of significance numbers as explained in detail below. At the same time, a technology forecast is made at the primary systems level and lower levels, aided by massive trend extrapolation and envelope curve techniques, as well as other forms of qualitative and quantitative exploratory forecasting. Apart from an identification of primary systems, secondary systems, and functional subsystems and their relationships, used for the relevance tree, two sets of characteristics are assessed explicitly: cross support, which means spin-off to other areas, or general technological growth to be expected from tackling a specific technical system; status (research, exploratory development, advanced development, product design, availability) and timing for systems and subsystems. These input data can be used in the computer programme if such refinements are desired; at present, Honeywell does not use cross support estimates (other than identical systems for different missions, etc.) and uses status and timing only to sort out all projects already well under way.

Honeywell's military and space relevance tree, in its 1966 form, looks like Fig. 4.15. The levels of the relevance tree correspond to levels of technology

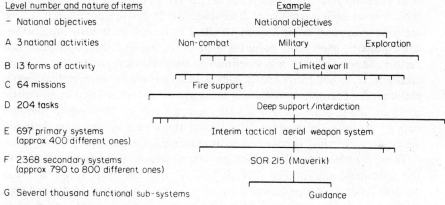

Fig. 4.15.

transfer between social systems (the nation) and technology or technological resources. In the technology transfer scheme used throughout this report, five to six out of the eight levels are covered by this relevance tree, a unique achievement so far for an integrated forecasting scheme!

Dynamic Modelling

This method involves the application of Forrester's ideas of industrial dynamics to forecasting*. Mathematical relationships describing the interactions are required involving feedback functions. The most dramatic illustration of this technique has been given in the book *Limits to Growth* by Meadows. Using feedback loops of the type shown below for world populations,

* Also discussed in Chapter 5.

it was shown how, without certain controls, the world could destroy itself soon after the year 2000.

The feedback loop structure that represents the dynamic behaviour of population growth is given in Fig. 4.16. On the left is the positive feedback

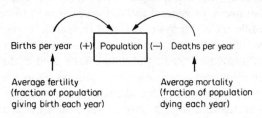

Births per year   (+) Population (—) Deaths per year

Average fertility   Average mortality
(fraction of population   (fraction of population
giving birth each year)   dying each year)

Fig. 4.16.

loop that accounts for the observed exponential growth. In a population with constant average fertility, the larger the population the more babies will be born each year. The more babies, the larger the population will be the following year. After a delay to allow those babies to grow up and become parents, even more babies will be born, swelling the population still further. Steady growth will continue as long as average fertility remains constant. If, in addition to sons, each woman has on the average two female children, for example, and each of them grows up to have two more female children, the population will double each generation. The growth rate will depend on both the average fertility and the length of the delay between generations. Fertility is not necessarily constant, of course.

There is another feedback loop governing population growth, shown on the right-hand side of Fig. 4.16. It is a negative feedback loop. Whereas positive feedback loops generate runaway growth, negative feedback loops tend to regulate growth and to hold a system in some stable state. They behave much as a thermostat does in controlling the temperature of a room. If the temperature falls, the thermostat activates the heating system, which causes the temperature to rise again. When the temperature reaches its limit, the thermostat cuts off the heating system, and the temperature begins to fall again. In a negative feedback loop a change in one element is propagated around the circle until it comes back to change that element in a direction opposite to the initial change.

The negative feedback loop controlling population is based upon average mortality, a reflection of the general health of the population. The number of deaths each year is equal to the total population × the average mortality (which we might think of as the average probability of death at any age). With rising health standards and food supply, world population has risen rapidly. In 1650 it numbered about 0.5 billion, and it was growing at a rate of approximately 0.3% per year. That corresponds to a doubling time of nearly 250 years. In 1970 the population totalled 3.6 billion and the rate of growth was 2.1% per year. The doubling time at this growth rate is 33 years. Thus, not only has the population been growing exponentially, but the rate of growth has also been growing. We might say that population growth has been super-exponential; the population curve is rising even faster than it would if growth were strictly exponential. The effect of this, if it continued, on supply, pollution, etc., is shown in Fig. 4.17. Using the dynamic modelling approach, various other assumptions are made to bring the situation under control as shown in Figs. 4.18 and 4.19.

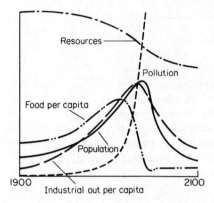

Fig. 4.17. World model with 'unlimited' resources. The problem of resource depletion in the world model system is eliminated by two assumptions: first, that 'unlimited' nuclear power will double the resource reserves that can be exploited, and second, that nuclear energy will make possible extensive programmes of re-cycling and substitution. If these are the only changes introduced, growth is stopped by rising pollution.

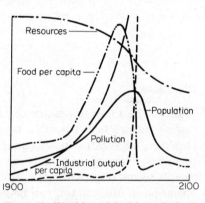

Fig. 4.18. World model with 'unlimited' resources, pollution controls, and increased agricultural productivity. To avoid the food crisis, average land yield is doubled in 1975 in addition to the pollution and resource policies. Combination of these three policies removes so many constraints to growth that population and industry reach very high levels. Although each unit of industrial production generates much less pollution, total production rises enough to create pollution that brings an end to growth.

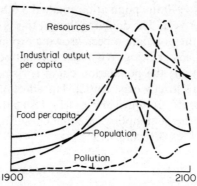

Fig. 4.19. World model with 'unlimited' resources, pollution controls, and 'perfect' birth control. Instead of an increase in food production, an increase in birth control effectiveness is tested as a policy to avert the food problem. Since the birth control is voluntary and does not involve any value changes, population continues to grow, but more slowly than it did previously. Nevertheless, the food crisis is postponed for only a decade or two.

Discussion

Many of the above techniques contain elements of planning as well as forecasting. In practice it is often necessary to combine these two processes. However, a forecast is strictly an input to the planning and decision-taking processes. Elements of forecasting are involved in any decision-taking process. It seems very reasonable to make explicit the forecasting part of the operation in order that it can be subjected to scrutiny and discussion, and also in order that a permanent record is available for subsequent comparison with actual outcomes. In this way the reasons for good or bad forecasts may become clearer and the ability to forecast may improve. It seems to us that poor data and information offer no excuse for implicit forecasting.

Although we have described techniques as subjective or objective, exploratory or normative, the ideal forecasts probably contain elements of all these in combination. It is a matter of judgement as to which is given the greatest emphasis, and so *all* forecasts have a subjective basis. It is as important to estimate, subjectively or objectively, the error of the forecast as the forecast itself.

Blind application of one of the mathematical techniques of forecasting introduced in this Chapter is a risk. In many situations there simply is not a long enough run of historical data available. If there is, changes in value of the parameter of interest may be explicable (for example, plant breakdown or an economic squeeze). It may be more appropriate to build a model that allows for these circumstances formally, and use this as a basis for forecasting. For example, Fig. 4.20 shows the number of secondary school pupils enrolled in Coventry Borough from 1946 to 1972. The peak in the curve centring

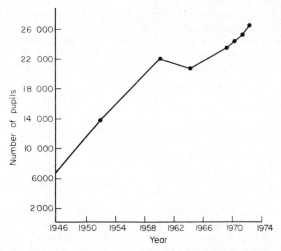

Fig. 4.20. Number of pupils enrolled in Secondary Schools.

on 1960 is due to the 'bulge' in the birth-rate following the second world war. Extrapolation to 1960 of school numbers for 1946 would produce a forecast error of about 4000 in 1964. Thus school-building programmes to accommodate these additional pupils could have been established quite unnecessarily from the early trend. A different model is required, based on the simple fact that present school numbers of age n years are strongly related to the number of births in year 'now' minus n. This demonstrates the importance of choosing the forecasting model most appropriate to the real situation. The techniques described in this chapter illustrate the choice available.

REFERENCES

Abt Associates, Inc., *Great World Issues of 1980*, Cambridge, Mass., April 1965.
Battersby, A., *Sales Forecasting*, Cassell, 1968.
Box, G.E.P. and Jenkins, G.M., *Time Series Analysis, Forecasting and Control*, Holden Day, San Francisco, 1970.
Calder, Nigel (Ed.), *The World in 1984*, The Complete New Scientist Series, Penguin Books, 1965.

Churchman, C.W., Ackoff, R.L. and Arnoff, E.L., *Introduction to Operations Research*, Wiley, 1957.
Forrester, J.W., 'Industrial Dynamics', *Harvard Business Review*, July-August 1958.
Gabor, Dennis, *Inventing the Future*, Secker and Warburg, London, 1963.
Gordon, T.J. and Helmer, Olaf, 'Report on a Long-Range Forecasting Study', Report P-2982, The Rand Corporation, Santa Monica, California, Sept. 1964.
Helmer, Olaf, 'Social Technology', Report P-3063, The Rand Corporation, Santa Monica, California, Feb. 1965.
Meadows, Donella H., Meadows, Dennis L., Randers, Jorgen and Behrens III, William W., *Limits to Growth*, Earth Island, London, 1972.
Thomas, R.E. and McCrory, R.J., *The Selection of Military Concepts for Long-Range Research and Development*, Battelle Memorial Inst., Columbus, Ohio, February 1964.
Zwicky, Fritz, *Morphological Astronomy*, Springer Verlag, Berlin, 1957.

BIBLIOGRAPHY

Brown, R.G., *Statistical Forecasting for Inventory Control*, Mcgraw-Hill, New York, 1959.
Brown, R.G., *Smoothing, Forecasting and Prediction of Discrete Time Series*, Prentice-Hall, Englewood Cliffs, 1962.
Cetron, M.J., *Technological Forecasting, A Practical Approach*, Gordon and Breach, 1969.
Davies, O.W., *Statistical Methods in Research and Development*, Oliver and Boyd, 1961.
Gregg, J.V., Hossell, C.H. and Richardson, J.T., *Mathematical Trend Curves, An Aid to Forecasting*, ICI Monograph No. 1, Oliver and Boyd, Edinburgh, 1964.
Forrester, J.W., "Industrial dynamics after the first decade," *Management Science*, Vol. 14, No. 7, 1968, pp. 398–415. *Morphology of Propulsive Power*, Monographs on Morphological Research No. 1, Society for Morphological Research, Pasedena, California, 1962.
Pearce, C., *Prediction Techniques for Marketing Planners*, Associated Business Programmes Ltd., London, 1971.
Wagle, B.V., 'Some techniques of short-term sales forecasting,' *The Statistician*, Vol. 16, No. 3, 1966.

5 Simulation and Monte Carlo Methods

We are, in truth, more than half what we are by imitation.
The great point is to choose good models and to study them with care.

Lord Chesterfield, Letters, 18 Jan. 1950

All the previous chapters have described *mathematical* methods of dealing with situations involving uncertainty. We must now consider situations that are so complicated as to defy mathematical analysis or so large that we cannot solve the resulting mathematical expressions.

Consider the situation of an engineer having to design the facilities for a new port. First of all he has to know something about the sort of ships that will enter the port, their cargoes, arrival patterns (which we have already discussed when looking at queuing theory), size of ship, etc., and a whole host of things that the port has to interface. Next he has to look at the service facilities that he can provide. What sort of cranes to unload the ships, their types, speeds, number? What kind of storage facilities? In sheds, outside, in frozen store? What sort of transport facilities to and from the dock, rail or road?

Another similar sort of example is the problem at airports of providing runways, baggage handling facilities, and customer liaison requirements. How is one of these items affected by the other? It is no good putting down a very expensive new runway unless you can manage to deal with the people at the terminal, and similarly it is no good having excellent underutilized facilities if the runway system cannot accommodate more aeroplane traffic.

Let us look again at the port example. Assume that ships arrive randomly with a mean inter-arrival time of 11.82 hours, the distribution of arrival times being as given in Fig. 5.1. This means that on average a ship arrives every 11.82 hours; but the time between arrivals could be as short as 5 hours and as long as 18 hours. The data about such arrivals will have been collected over a sufficiently long period to ensure that the figures are representative. The techniques to do this have been discussed in Chapter 2.

We have already stated that the arrivals are random. In other words, we

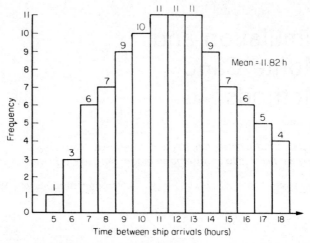

Fig. 5.1. Ship arrival distribution.

do not know the time of the next arrival but know that over a long period of time the arrival pattern fits. We would like to be able to 'generate' arrivals on paper as though they had really happened. But this means that any system can be 'lived through' painlessly on a piece of paper and all the possible outcomes understood before the scheme is tried out in practice.

In order to perform such an analysis we need to have access to random numbers. They are a series of numbers that have no pattern whatsoever and should have no relation to one another. The characteristics of such a series are that over a large set the digits 0 to 9 should occur with equal frequency, while ensuring that the neighbouring digits should have no relationship. For example, in the following set of numbers the digits occur with equal frequency:

```
0 1 2 3 4 5 6 7 8 9 0 1 2 3
4 5 6 7 8 9 0 1 2 3 4 5 6 7
8 9 0 1 2 3 4 5 6 7 8 9 0 1
2 3 4 5 6 7 8 9 0 1 2 3 4 5
```

However, it is obvious that they are not random – there is an easily observable pattern. So we have to generate the numbers very carefully to ensure that we have randomness; i.e. the digits 0 to 9 are equally likely to occur and there are no patterns whatsoever. In the early days, physical means of deriving digits were employed. For example, one device was a disc divided into 10 segments; this was spun by a motor and then arbitrarily stopped by the operator and the number of the segment under a fixed point taken as the next random number. Today random numbers can be obtained by a variety of means varying from compiled tables to calculation inside a computer. Many methods for testing for non-randomness have been devised and the current sources of random digits have therefore been fully tested.

Many simulations are so large that it is cheaper to use a computer, and in such cases an easy way of generating the numbers inside the computer would be an advantage. This is now usually done using a formula, where the next number depends on the last one. But such numbers cannot be random by definition, so they are called pseudo-random. By cleverly devising the formula and choosing its constants, it has been possible to develop a method that, to all intents and purposes, gives random numbers. However, for this exercise we will use a set of random number tables; their source is of little importance. A set of such numbers is given in Table 5.1; we will need to refer to them from time to time.

Table 5.1.   Random numbers.

10875	62004	90391	61105	57411	06368	11748	12102	80580	41867
54127	57326	26629	19087	24472	88779	17944	05600	60478	03343
60311	42824	37301	42678	45990	43342	66067	42792	95043	52680
49739	71484	92003	98086	76668	73209	54244	91030	45547	70818
78626	51594	16453	94614	39014	97005	30945	57587	31732	57260
66692	13986	99837	00582	81232	44087	69170	37403	86995	90307
44071	28091	07362	97703	76447	42537	08345	88975	35841	85771
59820	96163	78851	16499	87064	13075	73035	41207	74699	09310
25704	91035	26313	77463	55387	72681	47431	43905	31048	56699
22304	96314	78438	66276	18396	73538	43277	58874	11466	16082
17710	59621	15292	76139	59526	52113	53856	30743	08670	84741
25852	58905	55018	56374	35824	71708	30540	27886	61732	75454
46780	56487	75211	10271	36633	68424	17374	52003	70707	70214
59849	96169	87195	46092	26787	60939	59202	11973	02902	33250
47670	07654	30342	40277	11049	72049	83012	09832	25571	77628
94304	71803	73465	09819	58869	35220	09504	96412	90193	79568
08105	59987	21437	36786	49226	77837	98524	97831	65704	09514
64281	61826	18555	64937	64654	25843	41145	42820	14924	39650
66847	70495	32350	02985	01755	14750	48968	38603	70312	05682
72461	33230	21529	53424	72877	17334	39283	04149	90850	04618
21032	91050	13058	16218	06654	07850	73950	79552	24781	89683
95362	67011	06651	16136	57216	39618	49856	99326	40902	05060
95294	00556	70481	06905	21785	41101	49386	54480	23604	23554
66986	34099	74474	20740	47458	64809	06312	88940	15995	69321
80620	51790	11436	38072	40405	68032	60942	00307	11897	92674
55411	85667	77535	99892	71209	92061	92329	98932	78284	46347
95083	06783	28102	57816	85561	29671	77936	63574	31384	51924
90726	57166	98884	08583	95889	57067	38101	77756	11657	13897
68984	83620	89747	98882	92613	89719	39641	69457	91339	22502
36421	16489	18059	51061	67667	60631	84054	40455	99396	63680
92638	40333	67054	16067	24700	71594	47594	03577	57649	63266
21036	82808	77501	97427	76479	68562	43321	31370	28977	23806

The distribution of arrivals in Fig. 5.1 tells us how the ships arrive overall, but we want to look at individual arrivals. From the figure we know that for 9% of the occurrences the time between arrivals will be 9 hours, for 10% of the time it will be 10 hours, etc. and the total frequency adds up to 100. Let us allocate all the numbers from 00 to 99 inclusive over the distribution as shown in Fig. 5.2. These do not have to be just 100 numbers in the boxes, but it aids the subsequent explanation.

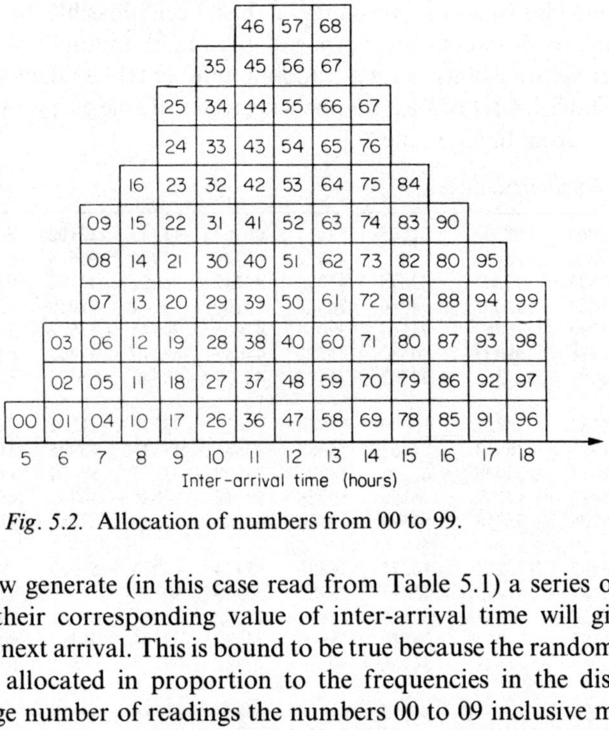

```
                        46 57 68
                     35 45 56 67
                  25 34 44 55 66 67
                  24 33 43 54 65 76
               16 23 32 42 53 64 75 84
            09 15 22 31 41 52 63 74 83 90
            08 14 21 30 40 51 62 73 82 80 95
            07 13 20 29 39 50 61 72 81 88 94 99
         03 06 12 19 28 38 40 60 71 80 87 93 98
         02 05 11 18 27 37 48 59 70 79 86 92 97
      00 01 04 10 17 26 36 47 58 69 78 85 91 96
       5  6  7  8  9 10 11 12 13 14 15 16 17 18
            Inter-arrival time (hours)
```

Fig. 5.2. Allocation of numbers from 00 to 99.

If we now generate (in this case read from Table 5.1) a series of random numbers, their corresponding value of inter-arrival time will give us the time of the next arrival. This is bound to be true because the random numbers have been allocated in proportion to the frequencies in the distribution. Over a large number of readings the numbers 00 to 09 inclusive must occur $10/100 \times 100 = 10\%$ of the time, just as happens in practice.

In order to make it more explicit we can take the first ten random two-digit numbers from Table 5.1. We have chosen to go from left to right instead of down the page, but it does not matter which method you choose as long as the method is systematic and not repetitive. Below we have put the numbers with the corresponding arrival times beneath.

Position	1	2	3	4	5	6	7	8	9	10
Random number	10	87	56	20	04	90	39	16	11	05
Inter-arrival time	8	16	12	9	7	16	11	8	8	7

The first random number is 10 and therefore the first ship arrives after eight hours. The next random number is 87 and this corresponds to an inter-arrival time of 16 hours, meaning that the ship arrives after 24 hours. This process can be repeated indefinitely.

Assuming we are starting at time zero we can now plot the arrivals on a cumulative time scale (Fig. 5.3). We have generated a series of arrivals that are, for all our purposes, no different from arrivals that actually happened. They come from the same arrival distribution and cannot be distinguished from them. We can now play with our paper ships at very little cost.

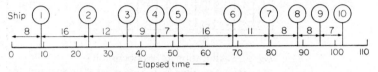

Fig. 5.3. Plot of arrivals on cumulative time scale.

Once the ships arrive they have to be unloaded. In this case we have only one berth and one crane operating. The time taken to unload a ship varies considerably, depending on such factors as ship size, type of cargo, crane breakdowns, etc. Not to make life too complicated, we will assume that all these factors can be incorporated into an unloading time distribution as shown in Figs. 5.4 and 5.5. This is a great simplification of course, and in a real life case such an assumption would be unwise, but for the purposes of our illustration it will be valuable.

We now have the information on which to base our simulation exercise,

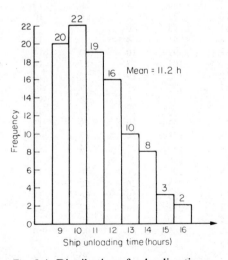

Fig. 5.4. Distribution of unloading times.

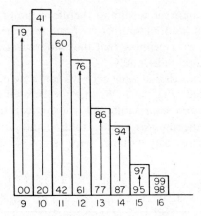

Fig. 5.5. Allocation of numbers for
ship unloading time distribution.

Table 5.2. Calculations for hand simulation of port operations.

Ship	Arrival				Unloading			
	Random No.	Inter-arrival time	Arrival time	Queuing time	Random No.	Unloading time	Departure time	Total time in port
1	10	8	8	0	54	11	19	11
2	87	16	24	0	12	9	33	9
3	56	12	36	0	75	12	48	12
4	20	9	45	3	73	12	60	15
5	04	7	56	4	26	10	70	14
6	90	16	72	0	26	10	82	10
7	39	11	83	0	62	12	95	12
8	16	8	91	4	91	14	109	18
9	11	8	99	10	90	14	123	24
10	05	7	105	17	87	14	137	31
11	57	12	118	19	24	10	147	29
12	41	11	129	18	47	11	158	29
13	10	8	137	19	28	10	168	29
14	63	13	150	18	87	14	182	32
15	68	13	163	19	79	13	195	32
16	11	8	171	24	17	9	206	33
17	74	14	185	21	94	14	220	35
18	81	15	200	20	40	10	230	30
19	21	9	209	21	56	11	241	32
20	02	6	215	26	00	9	250	35
21	80	15	230	20	60	11	261	31
22	58	13	243	18	47	11	272	29
23	04	7	250	22	80	13	285	35
24	18	9	259	26	33	10	295	36
25	67	13	263	32	43	11	306	
	Average	10.8 hours			*Average*	11.6 hours		

All we have to do is sample ship arrivals and sample the time it takes to unload, making sure that no more than one can be unloaded at once. Using the random number table provided, we have sampled the arrival of 25 ships, and we keep the information in tabular form as shown in Table 5.2. Here we have a list of all the times sampled and a cumulative total of the duration of the simulation. In fact the whole of the hand simulation can be progressed in this tabular fashion, but in general it is always useful to have a diagram of the event as well. We have drawn this in Fig. 5.6, and, by using both the table and the figure, it is easy to keep track of things. Let us now look at the simulated port.

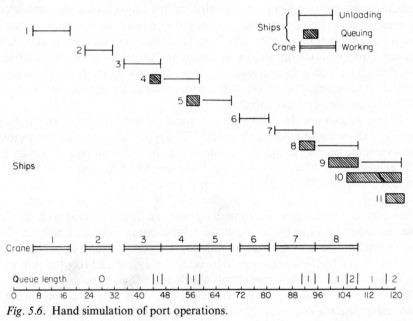

Fig. 5.6. Hand simulation of port operations.

Our first ship arrives after 8 hours. Assuming the port to be empty, we can start unloading–it takes 11 hours, and therefore the first ship leaves port at time 19 hours. The second ship arrives 16 hours after the first, at time 24. By this time the first ship has finished unloading and has left, and therefore it too can start unloading and it is found to take 9 hours. The next ship arrives at time 36 hours, and since the dock is unoccupied it does not have to wait. It commences unloading at time 36 hours, takes 12 hours, and is ready to leave at time 48. Ship four arrives at time 45, but finds that ship three is still unloading and does not finish until time 48. Therefore it has to wait, i.e. queue for 3 hours before it can dock. Similarly, ship five has to queue for a while. The simulation is progressed in this manner by sampling events (arrivals) and progressing them logically through the system. A queue starts to build up with ships eight, nine, ten, and eleven because of a few arrivals fairly close together.

As time passes a small queue builds up and stays for the rest of the simulation. Each of the ships has to wait for about 30 hours before it begins unloading. Is this what you would expect? In this case it looks reasonable because the rate of arrival is not much lower than the rate of service, i.e. 11.82 hours inter-arrival time against 11.2 hours on average to unload each ship. (Remember our discussion on queuing theory in Chapter 3.) The crane can just about cope but the ships have to wait. In fact, too much should not be read into the small simulation we have run. Only 25 ships have been considered and the sample size is much too small. One has only to look at the simulated average times of 10.8 hours inter-arrival and 11.6 hours on average to unload each ship. These ships have been arriving faster than they have been unloaded, hence a queue builds up. Before analysing the results of such a simulation, we must have run it long enough to cover the possibility of 'false' results from bad sampling. For anyone interested, continue the simulation for up to 100 arrivals and see what happens.

Before we can use the results of our model solution, we must also test its validity. Does it give reasonable results? This is always a problem and must be overcome before changing the simulation. In our example, for instance, the average times of waiting and unloading should be compared with actual practice. If they differ at all markedly, the simulation is not accurately modelling the process and needs revision. Similarly, if it is giving queue lengths far above those found in practice something is amiss. By performing such checks we can often find out more about the system being studied. For example, let us say that the average waiting time for the ships is found to be less than that produced by the simulation. Why is there a difference? It could turn out that the arrivals are not completely random and we have not spotted it. Maybe the arrival pattern is also correlated with cargo size etc., which would also affect the waiting time. Another solution might be that under periods of high activity the men forgo their lunch break and hence increase the unloading rate. There are many possible answers and these would vary in differing circumstances. The point we are making is that unless the model describes adequately the characteristics of interest it will be of little value for prediction purposes. Anyone can get answers, numbers, solutions, etc., from simulations, but they may be of little use unless the model has been validated. This phase of the process is of vital importance and is part of the simulation building itself. It is rare to be able to construct a model straightaway without some initial mistakes, which need correcting. In order to build a complex simulation, we require strict validation methods before the output can be at all meaningful.

To use the information from the simulation we have to ask ourselves 'What are we going to do with it?'. This question should be answered before starting the analysis and is sometimes forgotten by both the O.R. worker and the manager. In this case we are trying to operate the port as cheaply as possible. We have to pay the port's fixed costs, its operating costs, and the cost of keeping ships waiting. This last cost is called demurrage and may be quite high (a few hundred pounds an hour for a large bulk carrier). By increasing the number of cranes or using faster winches, the turnround of ships can be speeded up–thus lowering the queuing cost–but the operating costs are increased. In order to find the best policy to adopt, the simulation has to be carried out a number of times and the results analysed to see the effect of changing service rate, arrival rate, etc. Because this is usually necessary, in most cases today we would use a computer to perform the calculations. This would ensure that we could simulate long enough so that our results would not be due to an unusual sample and that we could re-run the simulation many times with little effort.

We now know how Monte Carlo simulations are carried out, and there are no difficulties in understanding the basic reasoning behind the analysis. However, the problem can arise of describing the logic of some operating system. For example, we took great liberties with the port problem. A very detailed description of a large realistic model of a port is given by Lawrence. In real life, simulation will provide some understanding of how complex factors interact, but it will not make the complexity go away. A large interlocking network of machines/services which interact and affect each other will probably require a large amount of effort if the decision rules operating within the system are to be understood. Many studies have been made in steelworks, airports, transportation networks, and machine shops, which have shown how great savings in operating costs can be made. But, before discussing such a case, it should be borne in mind that simulation is also applicable to much smaller problems, e.g. a study of the customer service in a cafeteria, or maintenance crews queuing for spare parts at the stock despatch. In such cases hand simulation may be appropriate.

One common occurrence in O.R. work is to find that people's first impression of a problem is not correct, and one of the tasks of an O.R. worker is to understand for himself what the real problem is. A very useful technique for a manager who feels he has a congestion problem, and which can help to establish whether the problem is real or not, is the method of random observation studies, often called ratio delay by production engineers.

It may be reported for example that a certain machine in a factory is always a bottleneck. To establish the facts for himself, the manager should merely note, each time he walks through the factory (which, except for meal times, will probably be at random intervals), whether the machine is in use or not. At the end of a fortnight, when he consults his records, he may be surprised to find that the machine is by no means in constant use as had been claimed. Armed with such facts, collected without special effort, the manager will be on the way to sorting out the real problem. Is it worth spending any money and effort on an investigation? In many cases it is not, but it obviously is worth it when we consider the problem of an integrated steelworks development, as below.

A complex plant

The problem arose when an old works was about to be modernized and a new steelmaking plant was to be introduced, along with other equipment. Liquid iron is produced at one end of the steelworks in blast furnaces, from which it flows at about 400 tons every 4 hours, although there is a lot of variation in the amount of 'hot metal' produced and the time between castings. It is impossible to get control of this variation completely owing to the inherent nature of the blast furnaces, and so we must expect large variations in the time and amounts of metal supplied. Because of such variations we require a buffer stock between this and the next process which is the melting shop where iron is converted into steel.

The buffer stock was established by having a number of movable rotatable vessels, known as torpedoes, which store the hot liquid iron. Each of these vessels could store about 170 tons of iron, but this varied from about 100 to 200 tons depending on how long the lining of the vessel had been in use. Costing of the order of £100 000 per vessel, the total storage capacity becomes an important cost item. If all the torpedoes became full, the iron from the blast furnace had to be poured into open-topped ladles, cast in sand, and allowed to cool. This reduced the amount of iron available temporarily and also incurred a large cost of heating up the solid metal again, by putting it back through the blast furnace. This action was not one to be done very frequently.

When a steel furnace requests metal it is poured from a torpedo into a ladle inside a pit. The ladle is then lifted by a crane and emptied into a steel furnace. Differing amounts of metal are required depending on the size of furnace, type of steel to be made, amount of cold scrap to be used, etc. In this case about 150 tons of hot metal were used each time. Two furnaces were to be in operation in the plant, acting completely out of phase. Some variation in the time between metal demands (known as tap to tap time) was expected, but the scale was much less than that of the blast furnaces.

The furnace pours its steel into a ladle under the furnace, and this is then emptied into a series of ingot moulds on a train. This train is moved to another part of the works where the ingots are removed from the moulds. The ingots are then put into a series of large ovens, called soaking pits, where they are allowed to remain for a while to achieve a uniform temperature throughout. After many hours they are taken from the pits and processed through the rolling mills.

If for some reason there are not enough hot ingots coming along to fill the pits – for example during a furnace breakdown – cold ingots can be placed in the soaking pits but they take a much longer time before they are ready to roll. Such a decision is rather important since it means that the rate at which the hot ingots can be accepted is reduced for a while, unless some of them are allowed to cool.

The whole system is a series of interlocking operations with buffer stocks in between, and it has only been possible here to give an indication of the size and scale of the operations. Anyone unfamiliar with such a large basic industry would find Collcutt interesting reading. Fig. 5.7 shows what we have been discussing in a diagrammatic fashion. As we have seen, the cycle of operations is very complicated.

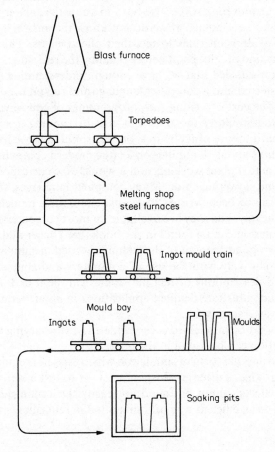

Fig. 5.7. Process of making ingots.

Any breakdown or delay from the blast furnaces may eventually lead to a complex scheduling problem at the soaking pits. Using a very large number of torpedoes, i.e. providing a large buffer stock between the blast and steel furnaces, would help matters but would be very costly. There is also another problem that has not yet been mentioned. The iron gradually cools and after a while has to be used or poured out of the vessels, so there is a limit to the buffer stock capacity. This is quite different from the sort of stock control problem we shall be looking at later on, and needs a different approach.

The problem was solved using a Monte Carlo simulation of the operations. First a hand simulation was done to sort out the logic of the process. It is usually best to try it out on paper first before writing a computer programme, because one can quickly and cheaply find the places where decisions are necessary. These are the important points in the system. For example, if we are running out of iron, do we use more cold scrap which slows down the steel furnace, or wait for a while? We have to know the answer to such questions before we can simulate. If we do not know the answer, we can put in different sets of decision rules to test their effectiveness. This initial hand simulation is a kind of pilot plant before building the real thing.

When we are satisfied that we have enough understanding of the system it can be transferred into a computer language and run on the computer in a few minutes. The cost of writing such programmes of course varies with the complexity, and similarly the time and cost of running a simulation are related. It is hard to give exact figures, but the simulation we have described above would take about 10 minutes on a large modern computer to simulate a few months actual plant working, and it would take correspondingly more on a smaller and slower machine. Many computer languages, such as C.S.L. and G.P.S.S., have been written to enable simulation models to be built quickly and cheaply, and they are available on most computers. Much more detail on simulation can be found in the books by Tocher and Naylor. The first gives a very good account of the techniques used in simulation, and the latter deals exclusively with the use of computers and simulation models. Many detailed descriptions of real life studies can be found, and those by Eilon and Gluck illustrate detailed applications in an air terminal building and on a railway respectively.

The range of problems tackled is very wide and cases varying from marketing to production can be found in the references.

There is also another form of simulation which does not require the Monte Carlo method. This is often used when we want to test a series of decision rules, whose effects cannot be found out easily. Deterministic simulation, as it is known, is an efficient way of trying out different rules.

Deterministic simulation

A new machine shop was being set up to manufacture a certain product which needed a short delivery time if it was to sell in adequate quantity. The manufacturing techniques and machining times for this product were well known, but it was necessary to determine as accurately as possible how many machines and men would be required to achieve a given throughput time with a known level of input. It was necessary also to determine whether men were likely to be idle for long periods if the input to the shop fluctuated, so that other work could be planned for them.

In other words, what was required was a model of the machine shop on which the manager could experiment by changing the number and type of machines, the number of men employed, and the input, and see what happened to work in progress, throughput time, labour utilization, and machine utilization, so that he could see where bottlenecks developed and plan how to eliminate them. The system was too complex for a mathematical model to be constructed and the whole shop was therefore imitated by means of an electronic computer.

To simplify the operation somewhat a 'first come, first served' production scheduling rule was assumed. That is, each job as it entered the simulated shop was dealt with in turn, and as each job finished on one machine it was placed on the end of the queue for the next machine. There were no priorities.

This is not an unrealistic picture. Priority rules, as every production controller knows, are the machine-shop manager's nightmare. For efficient working of a production unit it should be possible to produce everything within the time required on a 'first come, first served' basis. There must be exceptions, of course, as when a particular customer requires very quick delivery, but complex scheduling plans just will not work on the shop floor where machine breakdowns and absence of key operators through illness are not unknown. When a tight scheduling scheme is thrown out of joint by one such mischance it ceases to be operable.

One of the purposes of the simulation was to discover what the throughput time of various categories of parts was under the 'first come, first served' regime so that their scheduling and delivery dates could be arranged accordingly. A complex computer simulation was run on the plant, and we will describe the method below.

What the electronic computer did therefore was to take each job as it entered the 'shop', assign it to its first machine, and transfer it to its second machine when it had moved to the head of the queue on its first machine and had been 'operated on' for the appropriate length of time. This was done for each job on each machine until it emerged from the last machine as a 'completed part'. It should be stated that not every 'job' went on every 'machine' nor did each 'job' visit the same number of 'machines'. The total time taken from entering the shop to leaving it was measured, and at frequent intervals the length of queue on each machine was also measured. The numbers of men employed and men idle at any given time were also available.

Every time a man completed the processing of a job on a particular machine, a priority rule determined whether he should start on the next job waiting in the queue or move to another machine. Two-shift working was incorporated; the machines that were to gain or lose men at each change of shift were decided by the priority rule.

The manner in which the computer was used to simulate the operation of the machine shop will probably be clear if a simplified example is described. Consider a machine shop with six machines and three operators. Tables 5.3 and 5.4 show the times at which jobs are scheduled to be completed on the machines. Times are measured from the moment when the simulation started and are quoted as integral numbers, where the unit of time is one-hundredth of an hour.

Table 5.3 Position in queue

| | Position in queue | | | | |
Machine	(1)	(2)	(3)	(4)	(5)
A	2^{37}	2^{37}	2^{37}	2^{37}	2^{37}
B	13425	2^{37}	2^{37}	2^{37}	2^{37}
C	13049	13627	14308	2^{37}	2^{37}
D	$2^{37} + 13290$	$2^{37} + 13543$	2^{37}	2^{37}	2^{37}
E	2^{37}	2^{37}	2^{37}	2^{37}	2^{37}
F	13614	13901	2^{37}	2^{37}	2^{37}

Table 5.4.

| | Position in queue | | | | |
Machine	(1)	(2)	(3)	(4)	(5)
A	2^{37}	2^{37}	2^{37}	2^{37}	2^{37}
B	13425	2^{37}	2^{37}	2^{37}	2^{37}
C	13627	14308	2^{37}	2^{37}	2^{37}
D	$2^{37} + 13726$	$2^{37} + 13979$	2^{37}	2^{37}	2^{37}
E	2^{37}	2^{37}	2^{37}	2^{37}	2^{37}
F	13614	13901	14443	2^{37}	2^{37}

First, the computer is set to examine the jobs waiting at the heads of all the queues in order to locate the job that will be completed first. In the case shown, machine C will be chosen first because 13049 is the smallest number in column (1). The action now taken by the computer is, in effect, to move forward through time until it reaches the moment quoted, i.e. 13 049 units of time. This, of course, means that the operation on machine C will have been completed, so the job processed on this machine is transferred to the end of the queue of the next machine specified in the production sequence. This, say, is machine F and the job enters the third position in the queue. Suppose the time required to complete the particular operation on this machine is 542 units; the new completion time for this job is derived by adding 542 to the completion time given for the job immediately before it in the queue. The new completion time therefore becomes $13901 + 542 = 14443$. This figure is seen in Table 5.4. The queue of work on machine C is now moved forward, the number 13 627 coming to the head of the queue.

Only three operators are available to work the six machines; three machines must therefore be idle. Obviously, when the computer is scanning column (1) to detect the lowest number, it must be prevented from choosing a machine that is not manned. This is done by adding a very large number, 2^{37}, to the completion times of all jobs on unmanned machines. This number also appears in all positions in the queues not occupied by jobs. In this way it is possible to make the computer ignore all machines having no work (machines A and E) and also unmanned machines (machine D).

If the computer moved forward 436 units of time to get to 13 049, then 436 units must be added to the completion times of all jobs waiting in the queue of unmanned machines. This has been done for the two jobs waiting at machine D, and the new completion times are quoted in Table 5.4. All is now ready for the process to be repeated. The computer will search column (1) for the earliest completion time and the procedure will be gone through again.

A system of priorities is necessary to determine how the men shall be allocated to the machines. In real life this is a matter of intuition but, because the computer is incapable of exercising this faculty, a rule had to be found that would appear reasonable to workshop supervisors and could be programmed. The obvious rule of allocating men to the machines with the longest queues would penalize those jobs going on lightly loaded machines. The solution adopted therefore is to set a criterion of priority for each job by assessing the difference between the scheduled completion time for the job on its current machine and the time it joined the queue for that machine.

Whenever a job is completed on a machine the operator is sent to a central reserve. The computer then scans the jobs at the heads of the queues of the unmanned machines and allocates the man to the machine with the job possessing the highest priority on the basis just quoted. Of course, the machine the operator has just left has become inactive and, if it has a queue of work, it will often reclaim him. In this event, no break occurs in the operation of the particular machine because the computer does not move forward in time while it performs the allocation procedure.

In order that one programmed routine may be able to cope with the arrival of jobs at the machine shop as well as with movements from machine to machine, two special 'arrival machines' are included in the model of the situation. Each arrival machine has room for a queue of 48 jobs. If 97 jobs are placed in the queues of these machines the normal programmed procedure will see to it that they are fed into the workshop at the right times. A continuous flow of work is maintained by repeatedly feeding in a fixed sequence of jobs.

The data that need to accompany a job on its tour of the machine shop can be contained in two registers of the information store. Consequently, to provide sufficient information storage capacity for 48 separate jobs to be held in a queue, 96 consecutive registers were earmarked. (The number 48 has no particular virtue; it is dictated primarily by the storage system within the computer.) A maximum number of 40 machines was envisaged for the workshop, so 3840 registers were needed to hold their queues. Data which did not need to accompany the job on the journey from machine to machine were recorded in another part of the information store. Examples of such data are the reference numbers of the machines needed for the complete manufacturing cycle, arranged in sequence, together with the preparation times for each operation and the machining times.

Tables 5.3 and 5.4 illustrate the type of data recorded in the first register. The second register contained the priority value allocated to each job, the job number, and the number of machines that the job has visited. Without this last information it would not have been possible to look up the details of the next operation to be performed.

The simulation of the machine shop incorporated a means of periodically increasing and decreasing the number of men working in the shop. In this way shift working could be simulated. Both the length of the shifts and the distribution of manpower could be varied. Extra men were added to the reserve of free men on changing from night shift to day shift. These men were then allocated to machines, in accordance with the priority system already described, until either no more men were free or all machines with queues of work had received men. Conversely, the change from day shift to night shift involved, first, the removal of men from the reserve of free men; then, if further men had to go, they were removed one by one from the active machines with the lowest-priority jobs.

Every time the computer performed an action, a test was made to see whether it was time to print a report on the queues of work at each machine. These reports showed the forward load for each machine, i.e. the completion time of the final job in the queue minus the present time.

A simplified flow chart showing the main features of the programme appears in Fig. 5.8. The computer performed this cycle of operations approximately once per second. It can be seen that during a run most of the pro-

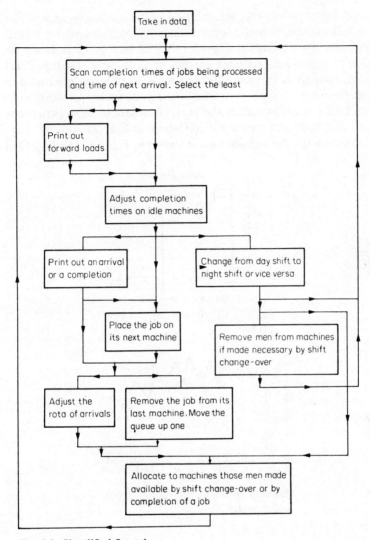

Fig. 5.8. Simplified flow chart.

gramme was used repeatedly. Those parts that were used only once were concerned with the introduction of data at the start of a run, or with stopping the computer when either a job was about to be loaded on to a machine that already had 48 jobs in its queue or a certain length of time had been simulated, for example 2000 working hours. Incidentally, the computer could simulate 10 hours operation of the machine shop in a few seconds.

Thus the model in the electronic computer was able to provide all the data that the manager needed to assess the necessary size of the machine shop, and gave him advance information of the conditions he was likely to meet. A fuller description of this particular simulation is given by Wyatt.

Typical results are given in Figs. 5.9 to 5.12. In Fig. 5.9 is shown the distribution of throughput time for batches of work under the input and output conditions given in Fig. 5.10. The work in progress generated by the average throughput time of approximately 2 weeks provided sufficient internal buffer stock to reduce the sharp fluctuations in weekly input to a much smaller fluctuation in output and labour utilization, shown in Fig. 5.11. The stability of the throughput time is shown in Fig. 5.12 in which the input

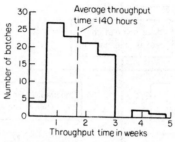

Fig. 5.9. Distribution of through-put time.

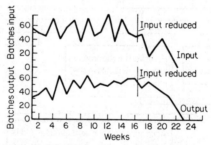

Fig. 5.10. Batches per week; input and output.

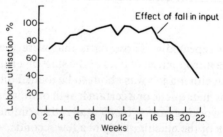

Fig. 5.11. Labour utilization; $4^1/_2$ week moving average.

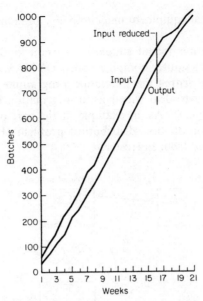

Fig. 5.12. Cumulative input and output of batches.

and output are plotted on a cumulative basis. This is a very useful method of observing the condition of a factory unit because the horizontal distance between the input and output lines at any stage gives the mean throughput time at that stage.

Where greater fluctuations in input than those shown in Fig. 5.10 had to be tolerated, the work in progress necessary to absorb these fluctuations and prevent excessive variation in labour utilization was readily calculable, as was the resulting increase in mean throughput time.

Electronic computer simulation of a complex production process is a very powerful O.R. tool for management. It enables the likely effects of many decisions to be estimated before they are taken so that harmful consequences are more likely to be avoided and beneficial combinations more likely to be observed.

Industrial dynamics

Another form of simulation Industrial Dynamics (see Forrester) was used in another context on p. 55. The method was derived to 'study the complex information feedback characteristics of industrial activity to how organisational structure, amplification (in policies), and time delays (in decisions and actions) interact to influence the success of the enterprise. It treats the interactions between the flows of information, money, orders, materials, personnel, and capital equipment in a company, an industrial, or a national economy'.

In essence it is a method of simulating certain kinds of total complex systems. A special computer compiler called DYNAMO has been written which is used when writing the simulation programmes. The package has facilities that allow it to deal with lags in information flows and works in terms of rates of change. As an example of the sort of problem tackled, consider a simple production distribution problem (Fig. 5.13) which is based on and adapted from Forrester.

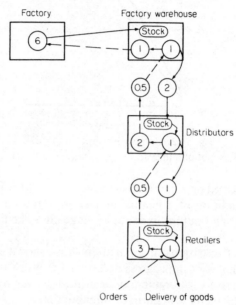

Fig. 5.13. Example of production–distribution chain.

Stocks of the goods (such as household appliances) are kept at three levels: factory, distributor, and retailers. The solid lines represent the shipment of goods, and the broken lines show the flow of orders for goods. This sort of organizational structure is typically found in industrial situations. In many cases there are time delays in passing the information from one level to the next, and it also takes time to manufacture and distribute. The numbers in circles are the 'delays' in weeks. Delivery of goods to customers takes on average 1 week after receipt of the order; it takes accounting and purchasing 3 weeks between the time of sale and the time when that sale is reflected in an order sent out to obtain a replacement; the factory takes 6 weeks to respond fully to a change in demand. We also need to know how the system operates its inventory policy. In this case we will assume that an 8 weeks average will be taken as the sales rate, and this is adjusted continually. After a sales analysis, and allowing for delays, orders to the next higher level of the system include replacement for the actual sales made by the ordering level. We have sketches of the basic dynamics of the system– but how does it operate in practice? The above system (like all systems) has its own special characteristics, and the results of changes of sales rates are not easily predictable without using some modelling facility.

Forrester has simulated the above system and we will now look at some of his results. The production-distribution chain is subjected to a 10% step increase in sales and some of the effects of this on the system are illustrated in Fig. 5.14.

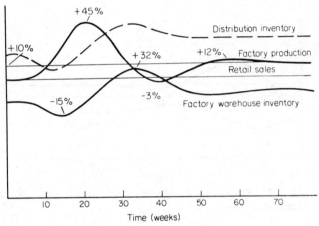

Fig. 5.14. Response of system to a sudden 10% increase in retail sales.

The curves show how factory production and some of the inventories respond to such a change. We have not included all the results of the simulation, such as the retail level inventory, goods or order, etc., but they illustrated dramatically the great fluctuations that occur because of the inherent dynamics of the system. The rate of factory production eventually (after 60 weeks or so) settles down to an expected increase of 10%. However, before that time it reaches 45% above 'normal' and drops to 3% below. Similar sorts of oscillations occur at other points via the chain–the more violent the further down the system from the retail (customer's) end.

Such sorts of reaction of an organizational system to change in the environment are not easy to predict. This simple example has shown that a 10% increase in sales at one end of a chain is accommodated by the system incurring almost violent changes in production. In certain cases the internal characteristics can sometimes lead to the amplification of small oscillations into large fluctuations in orders or output. We now have a method (a model) which we can manipulate, i.e. change the internal characteristics to find their effect. It is likely that the factory will not be very pleased with the present state of affairs and would like to see the production smoothed a little. Using the model, we could now estimate the effect of changing the delays to information flows (by improving the accounting procedures at some cost). One drastic method would be to cut out the distributor. If we did that, and neglecting the cost of changing (it could be positive or negative), the effect is shown in Fig. 5.15. The factory output now only rises to 26% above the original level rather than the 45% before (the broken line in Fig. 5.15). This sort of result raises the interesting question of whether the distribution set-up of some industries itself causes instabilities.

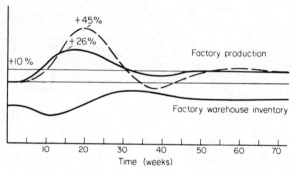

Fig. 5.15. Response of system when distributor is excluded.

One such example which comes quickly to mind is the market for disposable panties which started in 1967. The initial sales via one retailer were good and received attention by the press. Other retailers then requested the products, and production rapidly reacted to meet this demand. Essentially this was filling up the distribution chain, and not satisfying customer demand. The whole system oscillated violently and production 'collapsed'. In fact, production bore little relation to actual demand, and the suppliers were left with under-utilized production capacity. A small illustration of the dangers of misusing information in this way is given in the article by Lockett. Other industrial illustrations using industrial dynamics can be found in Wright and in Carlson.

Industrial Dynamics, or the principles behind it, have also been used to model very large systems. A new area of study called World Dynamics has been undertaken by Meadows and his colleagues, who have constructed models of the total world economy, population, resources, etc. They have been widely reported and argued about in the press because of their gloomy forecasts about the fate of the world. Whether or not they are right remains to be seen, but they have at least attempted to model some of the important parameters and interconnections of the world economy. Insights have been found about what are scarce resources, and you soon realize that, although all the nations of the world may be independent, they are interdependent.

Some of the Meadows results have been discussed in Chapter 4 with proper emphasis on the way in which the conclusions depend upon the initial assumptions.

Simulation is an efficient method of rapidly checking how this relationship affects any particular system under study, and it is thus a valuable technique in the armoury of Operational Research workers involved in corporate or strategic planning.

REFERENCES

Carlson, R.C., "Better schedules–automatically," IEEE Trans. on Engineering Management, Vol. EM-15, No. 4. December 1968, pp. 188–192.
Collcutt, R.H., *The First Twenty Years*, BISRA, London, 1965.
Eilon, S. and Mathewson, S., "A simulation study for the design of an air terminal building," IEEE Transactions on Systems, Man and Cybernetics, Vol. SMC-3, No. 4, July 1973, pp. 308–317.
Forrester, J.W., "Industrial dynamics–a major breakthrough for decision makers," Harvard Business Review, July-August 1958, p. 37 also Vol. 37, No. 2 March-April 1959, pp. 100–110.
Forrester, J.W., *Industrial Dynamics*, M.I.T. Press, Cambridge, Mass., 1961.
Gluck, R., Heissenbuttel, E. and Hillman, H., "Model railroading: simulation may make commuters love the LIR," *Computer Decisions*, Vol. 2, No. 8, August 1970, pp. 32–35.
Lawrence, P.A., "A computer simulation model for port planning," *Physical Distribution*, 4, 1; 1973, pp. 26–39.
Lockett, A.G. and Armstrong, K.N., "Throwing away millions–long range planning for disposables," *Long Range Planning*, September 1971, pp. 15–23.
Meadows, Donella H., Meadows, Dennis L., Randers, Jorgen and Behrens III, William W., *The Limits to Growth*, Earth Island, London, 1972.
Naylor, T.H., Balintfy, J.L., Burdick D.S. and Chu, K., *Computer Simulation Techniques*, Wiley, New York, 1966.
Tocher, K.D., *The Art of Simulation*, E.U.P., London, 1963.
Wright, R.D., "An industrial dynamics implementation, growth strategies for a trucking firm," *Sloan Management Review*, Fall 1971, pp. 71–85.
Wyatt, J.K., *Prediction by Computer Data Processing*, Vol. 1, No. 3, 1959.

BIBLIOGRAPHY

Guest, G. and Tocher, K.D., "The Control of Steel Flow," IFORS Conference, Oslo, 1963 (Paris, 1964)
Michael, C.G., "A computer simulation model for forecasting catalogue sales," *Journal of Marketing Research*, Vol. 8, May 1971, pp. 224–229.

6 Stock and Production Control Models

A place for everything and everything in its place.

Samuel Smiles, Thrift

Excessive stock has always been one of industry's main headaches. Many a managing director or plant manager must feel that if he could reduce his stocks he would have more money available for expanding his business and maybe more room to do it in.

There are really two problems to be considered. One is to decide what should be the minimum stock level of any component at which a fresh order for that component should be placed. The other problem is to decide what amount to order when the order is placed, (a) when one is purchasing from an outside supplier, (b) when one is manufacturing the item oneself.

Minimum Stock Control Levels

The problem of minimum safety stock or minimum re-order stock level, whatever one likes to call it, has been tackled in a variety of ways by O.R. workers. The problem arises because there is a delay between ordering the goods and receiving them and one needs a stock to cover sales during this delay. If sales were at a constant and predictable rate and delivery were assured in a certain time, then there would be no difficulty. The re-order stock level would be the exact amount of stock needed to provide for the quantity sold during the delivery period.

It is when both the sales rate and the delivery period vary that the difficulties become acute. If one held just enough stock to cover the average rate of sales during the average delivery period, it is not difficult to see that, because about half the sales rates would be above the average and about half the delivery periods would also be above the average, in approximately 50% of the cases the above amount of stock would not be sufficient and would be reduced to zero before the order arrived. Very few companies would tolerate such a high occurrence of delays either in providing customers with their demands or in supplying other production departments with their requirements.

Thus stock in excess of what is required on the basis of average sales and average delivery times is carried. The smaller the risk of running out of stock the greater the stock that must be carried. Using the methods of mathematical statistics, it is possible, in any given situation, to calculate the size of stock to carry for given probabilities of running out of stock. When a manager is presented with a clear indication of what stock he must carry to reduce this risk to 1 in 500 or 1 in 1000 (probabilities which many stock controllers feel they would like to achieve), he is often able to reconcile himself to a risk level of 1 in 50 in order to adjust his safety stock to a reasonably economic level. This risk level of 1 in 50 can often be more cheerfully accepted when calculations show that even when a 'stock out' occurs fresh supplies are available within a day or so.

In fact surprisingly high risks can sometimes be run if the period of delivery of the items is relatively short. It must be remembered also that the risks apply only to the items being ordered. If only a small proportion of items is on order at a given time, the chance that any item is out of stock when a customer calls for it is very much less than the risk of a run-out on the items being ordered. The following figures illustrate this. In a warehouse providing some 2000 items ex stock, fresh supplies of each item were ordered from the suppliers on average every 10 months. At any time some 30% of the items would be on order, delivery being about 3 months. As a result of an O.R. study Table 6.1 was drawn up. This showed that the warehouse manager could operate a buffer stock policy which allowed 15% of the items on order to run out of stock before being replenished, while running only a 2% chance of offending a customer by not being able to supply immediately from stock.

Table 6.1. Operating characteristics for various stock-holding policies.

Level of buffer stock in terms of average monthly sales	Percentage of ordered items expected to be out of stock before delivery is obtained	Percentage of items out of stock at any given time	Average time for these items to be out of stock
One month	26.4	3.5	0.8 months
Two months	14.7	2.0	0.7 months
Three months	8.9	1.2	0.6 months

The statistical methods used to evaluate the level of stock needed to provide a given level of protection need not be very complicated. The Secretary of a small company once asked an O.R. consultant to look at the purchasing policy of a branch office. This office was selling goods retail which it purchased wholesale. Despite the fact that the wholesaler was prepared to deliver weekly and offered no discount for quantity, the branch office purchased goods in substantial quantities at somewhat infrequent intervals. Its operations on a particular product for the first half of a given year are shown in Table 6.2.

Table 6.2. Actual stock-holding during first half of year.

Week	Stock at end of week	Purchases during week	Sales during week
1	63	60	28
2	34	—	29
3	67	60	27
4	51	—	16
5	29	—	21
6	72	60	17
7	39	—	33
8	80	60	19
9	48	—	32
10	66	40	22
11	30	—	36
12	50	40	20
13	35	—	15
14	4	—	31
15	31	40	13
16	63	50	18
17	38	—	25
18	23	—	15
19	48	40	15
20	34	—	14
21	21	—	13
22	6	10	25
23	Nil	—	6
24	21	30	9
25	11	—	10
26	23	20	8

A frequency distribution of the weekly sales for the first half of the year is in Fig. 6.1. There was no seasonal bias in the sales of this product; therefore one could expect this same distribution to be approximately followed in the second half of the year. The chance of a weekly sale exceeding a given figure, say 40, can be mathematically calculated, but for simplicity it was assumed that no weekly sale would exceed 36 in the second half of the year. The risk of making this assumption is, of course, approximately 1 in 26, because in

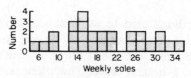

Fig. 6.1. Frequency distribution of weekly sales.

only one week out of the preceding 26 had a sale as high as 36 been realized.

Thus it was merely necessary to ensure that the wholesaler delivered weekly, and to order just the amount necessary to bring the stock at the beginning of each week up to 36. This would provide enough stock to meet all but exceptional sales in a week, and because delivery from the wholesaler was so short the consequences of any 'stock out' would not be serious.

The effects of trying this simple rule on the second half of the year in question can be seen from Table 6.3. It can readily be seen that the rule of starting each week with a stock of 36 means that the week's order from the wholesaler equals the previous week's sales. This illustrates the simplicity of some of the rules which emerge from an O.R. study. The actual behaviour of the branch office during the second half of the year (which was before the investigation was made) is given in Table 6.4.

There were no 'stock outs' under either system, but the average weekly stock which would have been carried under the O.R. scheme of Table 6.3 was 19, while that actually carried in Table 6.4 was 26. There was thus a

Table 6.3. Suggested stock-holding policy for second half of year.

Week	Stock at end of week	Purchases during week	Sales during week
27	26	13	10
28	20	10	16
29	19	16	17
30	25	17	11
31	25	11	11
32	28	11	8
33	13	8	23
34	28	23	8
35	20	8	16
36	22	16	14
37	4	14	32
38	17	32	19
39	28	19	8
40	23	8	13
41	13	13	23
42	24	23	12
43	13	12	23
44	19	23	17
45	16	17	20
46	19	20	17
47	23	17	13
48	8	13	28
49	15	28	21
50	20	21	16
51	10	16	26
52	18	26	18

Table 6.4. Actual stock-holding policy during second half of year.

Week	Stock at end of week	Purchases during week	Sales during week
27	33	20	10
28	17	—	16
29	20	20	17
30	9	—	11
31	18	20	11
32	30	20	8
33	7	—	23
34	19	20	8
35	23	20	16
36	29	20	14
37	37	40	32
38	18	—	19
39	20	10	8
40	37	30	13
41	14	—	23
42	42	40	12
43	19	—	23
44	22	20	17
45	42	40	20
46	25	—	17
47	52	40	13
48	24	—	28
49	3	—	21
50	27	40	16
51	51	50	26
52	33	—	18

saving of 27% to be made in stock level by taking a known risk of a 'stock out'. A similar study in a company stocking steel products has been reported by Collcutt and his colleagues.

This rationalization of stock levels with commercial risks is usually the first task of an O.R. worker in investigating stock problems, and the savings which can accrue are often quite substantial. A further advantage is that, when 'stock outs' occur in such a system, provided that they happen with the appropriate frequency, they are recognized as one of the expected consequences of the original management decision on stock levels. They do not become an opportunity to shower recriminations on the stock controller who, in the absence of such awareness, would seek protection in ever-increasing stocks.

Although emphasis has been placed so far on the determination of re-order stock level, the above considerations apply equally well to systems with a given re-order interval. Such systems have advantages in the ordering of components for assembly and have been discussed by Magee.

Re-order Quantities

The second problem, that of re-order quantities, is tackled in a somewhat different way. Again, two opposing commercial considerations are weighed against each other but this time probability does not enter into the calculation. The inherent variability of the system has already been taken care of in the chosen value of minimum stock level (re-order interval if the latter is used). The two considerations are, first the fact that one usually obtains the parts at a decreasing cost per item as the order size increases (this did not happen with the above example, hence the problem did not arise), and secondly the fact that the greater the order size the longer the parts remain in stock before being sold and hence the greater the storage and investment cost per item.

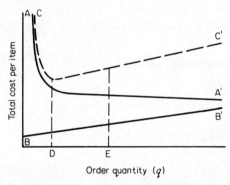

Fig. 6.2. Relation of cost to order quantity.

These two factors, the one decreasing the item cost, the other increasing it, can be represented graphically as shown in Fig. 6.2. Curve AA′ is the curve showing how unit cost decreases with order quantity. The straight line BB′ shows how unit storage and investment cost increases with order quantity, because, at a given rate of sale, the items remain in store for a longer period and thus take up space and require capital for a longer period. The broken curve CC′ is the sum of AA′ and BB′ and represents the change in the total cost per item with order quantity. It is seen that there is a minimum total cost per item at order quantity D, and this, in simple situations, is the quantity that should be ordered.

The minimum cost of queuing arises from similar considerations, see p. 34, emphasising the relationship between queuing theory and stock and production control. This quantity can be calculated in the following manner (non-mathematical readers may like to skip immediately to p. 94).

Let the fixed cost per order be c and the variable cost be m. Then the equation of line AA′ is:

$$\text{Manufacturing cost per item} = \frac{c}{\text{Order quantity}} + m$$

Let P be the interest and storage costs of the invested stock in per cent per month. In certain cases these can be calculated; in other cases, as explained later, they can, for the purposes of control, be any figure considered appropriate in the circumstances. This figure need not necessarily be the Bank Rate, or Dividend Rate, or Expected Return on Invested Capital, or any of the usual criteria.

Let S be the average monthly sales rate of the item ordered. The average time for which an item is in stock will therefore be:

$$\frac{1}{2}\left(\frac{\text{Order quantity}}{S}\right)$$

The interest that will be charged to the item for this period of time will be:

$$\text{Manufacturing cost per item} \times \frac{\text{Order quantity}}{2S} \times \frac{P}{100}$$

Hence the equation for line BB′ is:

Investment cost per item

$$= \left(\frac{c}{\text{Order quantity}} + m\right) \times \frac{\text{Order quantity}}{2S} \times \frac{P}{100}$$

If we let the order quantity (whose value for minimum cost we want to find) be x, then the equation of the line CC′ is:

$$\text{Total cost per item} = \frac{c}{x} + m + \left(\frac{c}{x} + m\right) \times \frac{x}{2S} \times \frac{P}{100}$$

$$= \frac{c}{x} + m + \frac{cP}{200S} + \frac{mP \times x}{200S}$$

The minimum value of this total cost per item, the point D, can be found mathematically, by differential calculus, to be where:

$$x^2 = \frac{200cS}{mP}$$

or

$$x = \sqrt{(200cS/mP)}$$

This is the well-known square-root formula, and it and its derivatives are bandied about by O.R. workers to a dangerous extent. It is safe to say that almost any ordering scheme which uses this formula will cause serious production difficulties in circumstances that will be discussed later, and will almost certainly result in an inflated level of stock being carried.

The economic justification for using the square-root formula is that by minimizing costs it maximizes profit. This justification needs closer examination. At first sight it seems appropriate because maximum profit is made from investments when the marginal return on capital is equal to the marginal cost of capital, and as shown below this equation gives the same square-root formula as before (again, non-mathematical readers may like to miss this proof):

$$\text{Cost per unit} = \frac{c}{x} + m$$

$$\text{Cost per batch} = c + mx$$

$$\text{Average capital investment} = \frac{c + mx}{2}$$

Let V be the selling price, then:

$$\text{Gross profit per unit} = V - \left(\frac{c}{x} + m\right)$$

$$\text{Gross profit per annum} = S\left[V - \left(\frac{c}{x} + m\right)\right]$$

$$\text{Rate of change of profit with quantity} = \frac{\delta\,\text{Profit}}{\delta x}$$

$$= \frac{Sc}{x^2}$$

$$\text{Rate of change of capital with quantity} = \frac{\delta\,\text{Capital}}{\delta x}$$

$$= \frac{m}{2}$$

Therefore

$$\frac{\delta\,\text{Profit}}{\delta\,\text{Capital}} = \text{Marginal rate of return on capital}$$

$$= \left(\frac{Sc}{x^2}\right)\bigg/\left(\frac{m}{2}\right) = \frac{2Sc}{mx^2}$$

To maximize profits:

Marginal return on capital $=$ Marginal cost of capital

$$= P/100$$

Therefore

$$\frac{2Sc}{mx^2} = P/100$$

$$x = \sqrt{\left(\frac{200\,cS}{mP}\right)} \qquad \text{(as before)}$$

If the shape of the curve of marginal rate of return on capital, as shown in Fig. 6.3, is examined, however, it is seen to fall sharply with increase of batch size and then to decline only slowly until it eventually crosses the line:

Marginal cost of capital $= P$

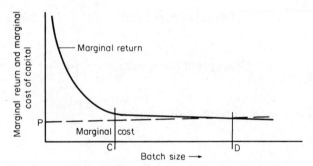

Fig. *6.3*. Marginal rate of return on capital.

at batch size D. The full line is the marginal return and the broken line is the marginal cost line.

Over the range of batch size CD the marginal return on capital is very little greater than the marginal cost of capital, and while this would not matter to a firm with unlimited capital, to a company with only a limited amount of capital, and most firms are in this situation, serious consideration should be given to whether further investment beyond C would not better be made in some other product where the marginal return on the capital invested would be higher than in the region CD.

The very small advantage to the company by increasing its batch sizes beyond C (say, half the quantity predicted by the square-root formula) can be shown in the following example (which can also be missed out by non-mathematicians).

Let $S = 100$ per annum, $m = £2$, $c = £10$, $P = 10\%$, and $V = £4$; then:

$$x = \sqrt{\left(\frac{200 \times 10 \times 100}{2 \times 10}\right)} = 100$$

The net annual profit is:

Average investment $\times$ (Average return on capital
$-$ Average cost of capital)

$$\text{Average investment} = \frac{£ (10 + 2x)}{2} = £ (5 + x)$$

$$\text{Average rate of return on capital} = \frac{£S\left[V - \left(\dfrac{c}{x} + m\right)\right]}{\dfrac{c + mx}{2}}$$

$$= £200\left(\frac{4}{10 + 2x} - \frac{1}{x}\right)$$

$$= \frac{400}{5 + x} - \frac{200}{x}$$

$$\text{Average cost of capital} = 10\% = \frac{10}{100}$$

$$\text{Net annual profit} = £ (5 + x)\left(\frac{400}{5+x} - \frac{200}{x} - \frac{1}{10}\right)$$

$$= £400 - \frac{200(5+x)}{x} - \frac{5+x}{10}$$

$$= £100\left(4 - 2 - \frac{1}{200} - \frac{10}{x} - \frac{x}{1000}\right)$$

With batch size x $= 100$:
   Average investment $= £105$
   Net annual profit $= £179.5$

With batch size $x/2$ $= 50$:
   Average investment $= £55$
   Net annual profit $= £174.5$

Thus, by using a batch size x in place of a batch size $x/2$, the capital employed is about doubled with a resulting increase in annual profit of only 3%. Most boards of directors could do better than this by doubling the amount of capital employed in their business.

The reason for this meagre result is that with a batch size of $x/2$ the £55 of capital earns a marginal rate of return of:

$$\frac{1000}{x^2} = \frac{1000}{2500} = 40\%$$

whereas, with a batch size of x the £105 of capital employed only earns a marginal rate of return of:

$$\frac{1000}{10\,000} = 10\%$$

as is to be expected since this equals the marginal cost of capital of 10%.

If there are other ways within the firm where a marginal rate of return greater than 10% can be earned, the batch size should be reduced below x so as to free capital for this use.

Thus, an uninformed use of the square-root formula can lead to batch sizes, and hence stocks, in excess of those that are in the best interest of the firm.

There are many other reasons why the square-root formula should not be used for fixing batch sizes. Many of the assumptions about set-up charges etc. underlying its construction just do not apply in practice. This has been forcefully pointed out by Burbidge.

When used to determine batch sizes in a factory, the square-root formula leads to production difficulties as pointed out by Salveson. Using this formula each item is ordered from the factory in proportion to the square-root of its own sales rate. However, each product will continue to be sold in direct proportion to its own sales rate. There will thus be a lack of balance between the order quantities of these different products and their rates of sale. This will not matter if the several articles represent only a small proportion of the plant's output, because then they will not get in each other's way. But if they do account for the bulk of the plant capacity then there will be occasions when two separate articles will need to be produced at the same time. This is impossible, of course, and the makeshift which will have to be introduced will cause departure from what was considered to be an optimum policy.

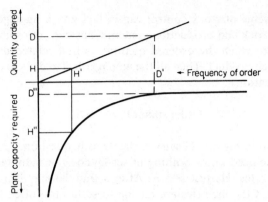

Fig. 6.4. Relation of plant capacity to order quantity.

Plant capacity is of importance too in deciding upon the optimum amount to order. The smaller the quantities the less the investment in stock, but a greater proportion of unproductive time is spent in setting up and orders have to be placed more frequently. It is shown by Fig. 6.4 that the plant capacity may not be sufficient to allow the order quantity to become too small.

The final choice, as in all such cases, is up to management.

This illustrates what was said in the introduction, that it is not the object of O.R. to usurp the decision-making function of a manager, it is to give it a greater scientific precision, a cutting edge. Thus, instead of worrying about which value to place on investment interest or chivvying accountants to provide it, the O.R. worker calculates several schemes based on different values of investment interest etc. and presents these to the manager who has to make the decision.

This manager has his own intuitive assessment of the level of investments which the company can carry and of the production cycle lengths that are economically acceptable. This assessment is based upon a host of intangible factors which no O.R. investigation can hope to tease out. The assessment will vary according to the economy not only of the firm in question but also of the country as a whole. When this assessment can be used to select one from a variety of schemes which the O.R. man presents, each of which is internally consistent, then the most fruitful and effective combination of intuitive and scientific insight has resulted. The manager knows at what level he wants his company or departments to operate. The O.R. man can ensure that it operates at this level consistently, and most people familiar with existing stock and production control schemes know that the bugbear is their inconsistency. Stocks of one part can be sky-rocketing, while panic measures are resorted to for obtaining enough supplies of another part.

An O.R. scheme of stock control can in fact give a manager 'finger tip' control of his stock and production system. Consider, for example, a simple order system in which the ordered quantity is best related directly to the sales rate of each product. Then all the manager has to do is to find the value of K in the equation:

$$\text{Order quantity} = KS$$

where S is the monthly rate of sales of the items in question.

To do this he need know nothing of set-up costs or manufacturing costs or investment rates. He just sets K. After a time he may learn that stocks are high, or that the factories are having to set-up too often for too small quantities, or that run-outs are frequent because of too frequent ordering. To correct the situation he merely alters the value of K. He will know, when everything is running smoothly, and factories, sales department, and accountants are satisfied (or dissatisfied), that he has chosen the right value. To aid him initially he could of course have a simulation carried out and choose the value of K that optimizes results in the simulation. The point is that,

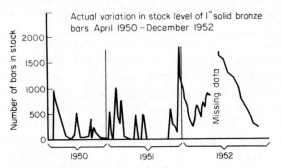

Fig. 6.5. Before O.R. investigation.

Fig. 6.6. After O.R. scheme.

once a scheme has been chosen which ensures consistency of ordering throughout the system, the parameters can be set by the controlling manager without the need for detailed cost or production studies, and these parameters can be changed at will to meet changing situations.

The results of giving a manager some quite simple schemes can often be very encouraging, as seen from Figs. 6.5 and 6.6 which illustrate the effect on one stock control system of the initiation of a simple O.R. plan whose level of operation was left to the manager concerned.

One precaution which must be observed when simple stock control schemes, such as those described, are inaugurated is that the effect of a change in the system should be examined. For example, the scheme in which items are re-ordered when a certain level of buffer stock is reached, and the order quantity is proportional to the sales rate, is subject to the acceleration effect. When sales increase steadily over a long period the buffer stock is reached more frequently and the order quantity increases each time that an order is placed. The combined effect of these two changes is to increase the total orders placed by more than the increase in sales. In fact, as sales increase the order volume is increased by the square of the increase in sales. When sales decline over a long period the opposite effect occurs. The result is illustrated in Fig. 6.7.

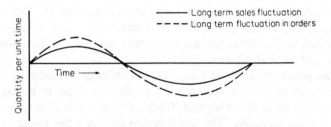

Fig. 6.7. Variation of orders relative to fluctuating sales.

Although this 'acceleration' of orders relative to sales may seem undesirable, especially if the goods are produced in the same organization that sells them, and it may therefore lead to overstrained resources, it is really the correct policy to pursue. This is because orders must always be placed in advance of sales, and if sales are continually increasing then the orders must be increasing faster in order that the goods will be in stock when required. This 'out of phase' effect is illustrated in Fig. 6.8.

The orders graph and sales graph are assumed to be identical in shape, as they should be if the order policy is sensible, but, because the orders graph must be displaced ahead of the sales graph, i.e. earlier in time, its gradient at a given point of time (say t), that is the rate of increase of orders with time, must be higher than that of the sales graph at the same time.

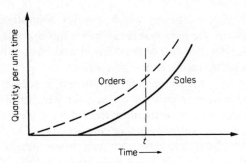

Fig. 6.8. Variation of orders relative to continually increasing sales.

Thus, if a factory expects its sales to increase at an accelerating rate over a long period, it must be prepared to produce goods at an even greater rate of increase if its delivery periods are not to lengthen. If it expects its sales to fluctuate over long periods as shown in Fig. 6.7, then either it must be prepared for even greater fluctuations in its work load or it must carry a strategic buffer stock to enable it to sell faster than it is producing for as long as the increase in sales permits. This stock can be replenished during the period of low sales.

This strategic stock is kept for different reasons from the tactical buffer stock that enables random fluctuations in sales to be coped with.

This example illustrates the use of operational research thinking in both strategic and tactical spheres.

The 'acceleration' effect is a well-known effect in industry; it can cause a minor boom in sales at one end of a productive chain to be experienced as a major boom at the other end. Contrariwise, a minor drop in sales can cause a serious recession. The solution depends on a full understanding of the causes of the acceleration and cooperation between all links in the productive chain in keeping either adequate stocks or adequate reserves of capacity. The problem has been very fully discussed by Forrester, who has developed the concept of Industrial Dynamics which we described at the end of Chapter 5.

Production scheduling

When the order quantities have been decided, problems may occur in scheduling these through the factory in an optimum manner. If the products form the bulk of a factory's or a department's output, quite complex methods may be needed to help solve the problem. In some cases linear programming methods have proved useful; in others a comprehensive simulation may have been used. But even the most simple situation may hide the most difficult problem. With nine products, for example, being made in one process there are more than 360 000 ways in which the order of manufacture can be arranged. Similarly, with five different products each requiring an operation on each of five different machines, the possible number of different sequences for scheduling the job is approximately 25 000 million, see p. 105. Of course, many of the possible sequences might be not worth consideration, but even so the number remaining is fairly large. It is impossible for any scheduling officer to consider all the combinations, and thus he cannot be sure that he has the optimum arrangement.

Operational research is finding solutions to some of these problems, however, and even when scheduling seems simple it is worth carrying out an investigation.

Consider nine products which require manufacture on two machines A and B successively for the times given in Table 6.5. In what order should the jobs be done in order to minimize the total time, bearing in mind that a job cannot transfer to machine B until it has finished on machine A?

Table 6.5.

Product	Time on machine	
	A	B
1	4	2
2	5	3
3	5	4
4	3	9
5	2	1
6	5	7
7	2	4
8	2	6
9	7	5

Table 6.6.

Job No.	Time of machine	
	A	B
7	2	4
8	2	6
4	3	9
6	5	7
9	7	5
3	5	4
2	5	3
1	4	2
5	2	1

It is shown in Fig. 6.9 that the order given in Table 6.5 is very wasteful of time because very often machine B is left waiting for a job to finish on machine A. The simple rule devised by Johnson to deal with this situation is as follows: Find the smallest machining time. If this is on machine B, put the job in question at the end; if it is on machine A, put it at the beginning. Then find the next smallest machining time and proceed in the same way by making the job concerned either the second or the second last. Where several jobs have the same smallest time rank them in order of the associated time on the other machine. In the case of Table 6.5 this will lead to the schedule given in Table 6.6. This schedule, as shown in Fig. 6.10, takes less total time than the original schedule of Table 6.5 and Fig. 6.9.

With this kind of elementary rule O.R. can often assist in scheduling even

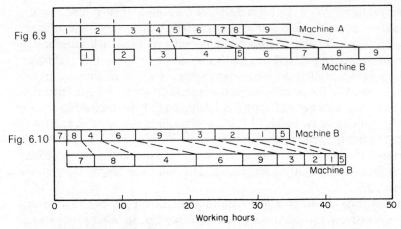

Figs. 6.9 and 6.10. Scheduling of nine jobs on two machines.

the simplest kind of production situation. This rule of Johnson's can be extended, with difficulty, to more than two machines, but it is not applicable for continuous scheduling, i.e. where jobs are continually coming into the shop, because then a product with a small machining time on the second machine might be put back indefinitely.

In the most general cases O.R. has not yet devised ways of finding the best sequence. But it has 'solved' many problems by using loading rules. These are 'heuristics' which are devices for getting good solutions, but not necessarily the best.

For example, a boiler maker has orders for four boilers, which must be finished in 36, 26, 31, and 33 days respectively. It is estimated that the four jobs will require the following times (in days) on the production machines:

Table 6.7

	Boiler			
	1	2	3	4
Cutting	1	2	4	5
Welding	2	5	3	3
Finishing	3	4	5	6
Painting	3	1	3	7

and we have only one machine of each type. What is the best manufacturing schedule?

The answer to this question is very difficult, because many factors have to be taken into account. A review article by Mellor points this out where he has a list of 27, including such things as lateness of jobs, machine utilization, etc.

As we stated earlier, it has proved impossible to find a method of getting optimal solutions. But some way of scheduling has to be devised. We will look at some typical loading rules that have been suggested, and see how they apply to this problem.

Consider the four rules below and let us schedule by choosing:

(1) the shortest processing time   (SPT)
(2) the longest processing time   (LPT)
(3) the due date of the overall job   (DD)
(4) the latest start time of the overall job   (LST)

First we have to calculate the quantities that we are going to choose from; they are given in Table 6.8. The processing times are just the sum of the times taken on each machine, and the due dates were given earlier. Latest start

Table 6.8

		Boiler		
	1	2	3	4
Process time	9	12	15	21
Due date	36	26	31	33
Latest start time	27	14	16	12

times are calculated by taking the processing time from its corresponding due date. For example, boiler 1 must be finished by day 36, it takes 9 days to make, and if it is not to be too late it must be started by day 27 at the latest.

Now that we have calculated the various quantities it is a simple matter to schedule. If we schedule by shortest processing time, boiler 1 is made first, followed by 2, 3, and 4, i.e. the schedule is 1–2–3–4. Scheduling by longest processing time produces the opposite schedule 4–3–2–1. As you can see these are all different, and to show this look at Figs. 6.11 to 6.14. The quickest schedules are given by the LPT and LST (29 days), whereas SPT takes 30 days and DD 32 days. Do not read too much into these figures for this small example, although the example does nicely illustrate the sort of differences that can occur.

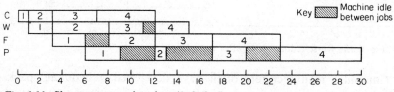

Fig. 6.11. Shortest processing time (1, 2, 3, 4).

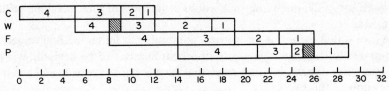

Fig. 6.12. Longest processing time (4, 3, 2, 1).

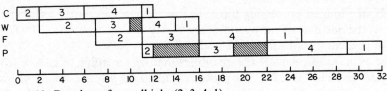

Fig. 6.13. Due date of overall jobs (2, 3, 4, 1).

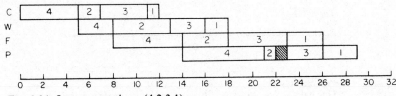

Fig. 6.14. Latest start times (4,2,3,1).

With a little more effort improvements can still be made. For example look at the LPT schedule. After 19 days it is possible to do some re-scheduling by changing over boilers 1 and 2. Both are ready to go on the finishing machine after boiler 3 has finished. If we put boiler 1 on first rather than 2, a new schedule is given which takes only 28 days overall, and Fig. 6.15 illustrates this. Much more detailed accounts of the effects of such rules can be found in the articles by Eilon. The 'rules' can become very complicated in certain cases, and some examples by Lockett and Muhlemann can be found in the references.

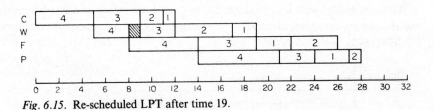

Fig. 6.15. Re-scheduled LPT after time 19.

Computer manufacturers often have developed 'scheduling' packages which they use on their own particular machines. Some of these have been successful, but they are mainly information processors. The actual sequencing of jobs is usually done using some weighted index number.

An example used by one company is to schedule on each machine by choosing the highest w, where w is given by a combination of weighted factors as shown here:

> value of item;
> external priority index;
> number of remaining operations;
> total remaining process time;
> last start time of operation;
> length of queue at next machine

These factors are converted to a common scale and multiplied by weights (constants) specified by the user. They are then added together to give a single number, w, and the machine is then scheduled by doing the job with the largest w first.

Such heuristics are not the main reason why the programmes have been found to be useful. The major benefit comes from the standardization of data, i.e. discipline imposed, and information processing capacity, i.e. keeping track of where everything is located, rather than the sequencing facility. This discipline is often the main advantage resulting from any O.R. study of stock and production control problems.

In this chapter we have illustrated a few of the approaches that O.R. workers have made to problems of production scheduling. We should remember, however, that we cannot look at production in isolation as a technical problem without considering the people who actually do the producing. The effect of changing stock operating policies may affect the system of production and hence the way people work. The saving in time by re-scheduling jobs on various machines may be beneficial to all the people within an organization, e.g. greater output, higher wages. In certain cases, however, the new schedule may require more flexible working procedures, e.g. men moving from machine to machine. If such factors have not been taken into account during modelling, the suggested courses of action may lead to unwanted results. Such behavioural aspects have not yet been modelled with any degree of success. Some of us might also suggest that their inclusion is not warranted, although recognition of their presence is vitally necessary.

REFERENCES

Burbidge, J.L., "A new approach to production control," *The Institution of Production Engineers Journal*, May 1958.

Collcutt, R.H., Banbury, J., Massey, R.G. and Ward, R.A., "A method of fixing desirable stock levels and of stock control," *Operational Research Quarterly*, Vol. 10, No. 2, June 1959.

Eilon, S., "Strategy and tactics in job shop scheduling," *Business Management*, April 1967, pp. 44–49.

Eilon, S. and Hodgson, R.M., "Job shop scheduling with due dates," *International Journal of Production Research*, Vol. 6, No. 1, 1967, pp. 1–13.

Eilon, S. and Cotterill, D.J., "A modified S.I. rule in job shop scheduling," *International Journal of Production Research*, Vol. 7, No. 2, 1968, pp. 135–145.

Johnson, S.M., "Optimal two and three-stage production scheduling," *Naval Research Logistics Quarterly*, Vol. 1, No. 1, 1954.

Lockett, A.G. and Muhlemann, A.P., "A scheduling problem involving sequence dependent changeover times," *Operations Research*, Vol. 20, No. 4, 1972, pp. 895–902.

Magee, J.F., *Production Planning and Inventory Control*, McGraw-Hill, 1958.

Mellor, P., "A view of job shop scheduling," *O.R.Q.*, Vol. 17, No. 2, June 1966, pp. 161–172.

Salveson, M.E., "A problem in optimal machine loading," *Management Science*, April 1956.

BIBLIOGRAPHY

Buffa, E.S., *Production-Inventory Systems: Planning and Control*, Irwin, Illinois, 1968.

Eilon, S., *Elements of Production Planning and Control*, Macmillan, London, 1962.

Nicholson, T.A.J., *Optimisation in Industry*, Vol. I and II, Longmans, London, 1971.

7 Resource Allocation

I'm very well acquainted, too, with matters mathematical,
I understand equations, both the simple and quadratical.

W.S. Gilbert The Pirates of Penzance

A series of techniques has been developed for helping in the solution of general resource allocation problems. The range of application is enormous but the basic problem is essentially the same, that of choosing from a large number of alternatives. For example, consider a machine shop which has five different machines, and we have five different jobs to be done. To make things easier assume that the processes can be done in any order; the number of ways that the jobs can be scheduled is $(5!)^5$, or approximately 25 000 million. Of course not all the possible combinations are worth considering. Probably there are also many technological constraints which we have not considered. These may restrict or complicate the choice, but even so the number of alternatives to be considered is often daunting.

There are many problems that have this difficulty of a large number of alternatives to consider, even though they may appear to have little in common: for example, choosing the correct mix of animal foodstuffs to meet certain specifications, choosing the correct mix of iron ores, or oils, or hides to make most profit. Similarly, the problem of transporting goods from warehouse to customer, or which oil tankers to send from which oil refineries, or which salesman to send to each customer are all problems involving large numbers of alternatives, i.e. they involve the problem of choice and someone has to decide. Some readable papers are listed in the Bibliography which cover some of the problems already mentioned. The sorts of situations listed above (and there are many more) have been tackled by a group of techniques which come under the general name of 'mathematical programming'. The range of application is now so large that it is impossible to do these techniques justice in a single chapter. Probably the most commonly used method is that of linear programming, and we will now look at a simple example. This will illustrate some of the essential concepts without getting very complex.

An interesting application is that of choosing the best hides to use in a tannery. Hides are the basic raw material and account for over 70% of the cost of the final product, leather. Various hides are available for purchase from most parts of the world. They vary in type (e.g. cow or ox etc.), thickness (which gives different types of leather), origin, and quality (e.g. number of brand marks and diseases), which all go to make up the price that is charged. Most hides are bought at auctions and hence there is often a problem of forecasting the prices. We shall, however, assume that prices are known.

Even so, the possible choice of hides may run from about 10 to 40 depending on time of year etc. It is not an easy task to decide which hides to buy, and a lot of money rests on the decision. When the hides have been bought they go through a series of processes which result in tanning itself. After this we can call the product leather, and there are still up to 20 production processes to be gone through to get the finished saleable product.

The first process after tanning is sorting and grading, where the leather is grouped into its final product category. Neglecting colour and graining finishes, there may be up to 10 product categories. Each of the hide types gives differing proportions when sorted – hence one of the reasons for price differences. The problem is to choose a set of hides that will give the correct amounts of leather required at minimum cost.

The constraints on the amounts of leather available have to be allowed for; the production process characteristics of each hide and leather must not be neglected, e.g. some hides require different production facilities. All these have to be taken into account, including the sorting proportions. As you can see, the possible complexity is beginning to look enormous and some method of helping in the decision would be very useful. Linear programming can be used to structure the problem and to sort the alternatives.

A number of companies now use the method in one form or another; we will only use the bare outline as a means of numerical illustration, i.e. we will neglect some of the complexity. Let us assume that there are two hides available for use, cow and ox, and that after tanning there are two grades of leather, A and B. The hide prices are different and the hides give differing proportions of graded leather. The details are as shown in the table and we require 20 grade A and 11 grade B leathers each day. What proportion of the two hides should we buy in order to minimize cost? For this small

	Cow	Ox
Proportion of grade A	50%	80%
Proportion of grade B	50%	20%
Hide availability per day	25	unlimited
Cost per hide (£)	10	12

problem you can probably guess the answer by applying a little arithmetic, but let us solve it by building a small model.

We wish to know the numbers of cow and ox hides to buy. These are our unknowns at present, and let them be x_1 and x_2 respectively. The cost of such a purchase is:

$$£ (10x_1 + 12x_2)$$

Fifty per cent of the hides from a cow make grade A leather. Therefore if we use x_1 cow hides this will make up $0.5x_1$ grade A leather. Similarly, x_2 ox hides gives us $0.8x_2$ grade A leather, and the total grade A leather is $(0.5x_1 + 0.8x_2)$. But we require at least 20, and this can be written as:

$$0.5x_1 + 0.8x_2 \geq 20$$

where the sign $\geq$ means 'greater than or equal to'. If we look at the requirement for grade B leather it is easy to derive in a similar manner that:

$$0.5x_1 + 0.2x_2 \geq 11$$

Finally, we have to express the limitation on the numbers of cow hides that are available each day, and this is simply given by $x_1 \leq 25$.

We now have expressed or 'formulated' the problem in mathematical terms, and have to minimize the cost, i.e. $10x_1 + 12x_2$, taking the following restrictions into account:

$$0.5x_1 + 0.8x_2 \geq 20$$
$$0.5x_1 + 0.2x_2 \geq 11$$
$$x_1 \qquad\qquad \leq 25$$

This is the formulation of a linear programming problem. Because we have only two hides (represented by variables x_1 and x_2) to choose from, we can use graphs to solve this particular problem. Consider the first constraint, i.e. $0.5x_1 + 0.8x_2 \geq 20$. The line AB in Fig. 7.1 has the equation:

$$0.5x_1 + 0.8x_2 = 20$$

Thus, all points on the line and to the right, as indicated by the arrow, have values greater than or equal to 20 and are in the region we want to consider. All points in the shaded area have insufficient grade A leather.

The second restriction, on grade B leather, is illustrated in Fig. 7.2 following the same reasoning.

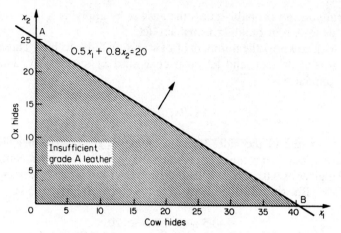

Fig. 7.1. Grade A leather restriction.

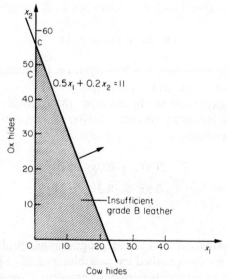

Fig. 7.2. Grade B leather restriction.

Similarly, the availability restriction $x_1 \leq 25$ is shown in Fig. 7.3.

The solution must lie in the unshaded region common to Figs. 7.1, 7.2, and 7.3. This is shown in Fig. 7.4 enclosed by the double lines. Within that region we want to choose the mix of hides at least possible cost, i.e. to make $10x_1 + 12x_2$ a minimum. The equation $10x_1 + 12x_2 = $ constant is also drawn on Fig. 7.4 where the cost is £400, i.e. $10x_1 + 12x_2 = 400$. This line represents different hide quantities bought, but keeping the total cost at £400. The

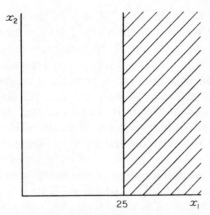

Fig. 7.3. Availability restriction.

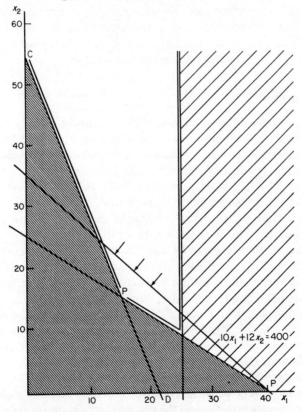

Fig. 7.4. Combination of Figs. 7.1–7.3.

slope of the line is constant, i.e. its alignment to the axes does not change, but the place where it cuts the axes depends on the value of the constant.

We would like to make this as small as possible. As we make it smaller the line it depicts moves parallel to itself in the direction indicated by the arrows. We could move the line until the constant becomes zero but the line would then be entirely in the shaded region – and the solution not possible. Keeping in mind that the solution must be in the unshaded region, the optimal solution can be seen to lie at the point P in the diagram. If we move any more we are out of the region. It can be seen that the solution is to use 16 cow hides (x_1) and 15 ox hides (x_2) at a minimum costs of $(10 \times 16 + 12 \times 15) = £340$. We do not therefore use all the cow hides that it is possible to buy.

A much more detailed description of the model used in practice in this example can be found in Lockett, where the history of the problem and implementation are discussed in some depth. We will come later to how the solutions to larger problems are calculated. The above example illustrates one of the most important facts about linear programming problems: the solution lies on the boundary or at the corners of the area of possible solutions. Therefore, when one has a much more complicated problem, this rule helps greatly in the search for the best solution.

An iterative method

What would happen if we had three hides to choose from, e.g. different grades of cow or ox, or hides from different parts of the world? This would require three variables to model the situation. We could just about model it using a three-dimensional construction, although we do not know of anyone doing it. If we have more than three we are into n-dimensional geometry and our simple graphical visual methods break down and we have to resort to a more mathematical technique. A very powerful but simple method of solution has been developed called the Simplex method. We will try to suggest how it works by using another illustrative example. This section requires a little more arithmetical manipulation. It should not prove difficult if you have got this far, but you may prefer to move on now to page 120 and leave this example for a later, more leisurely, moment.

A company makes three kinds of dart boards, of high, medium, and low quality, which use varying amounts of machine time and raw materials. Each high quality board takes 2 hours of machine time and uses 2 cork discs, a medium quality board uses 2 cork discs but only 1 hour of machine time, and each low quality board uses only 1 cork disc and takes up 1 hour of machine time. Every week the company has 1000 hours of machine time and 1600 cork discs available, and the marginal profits on the three products of high, medium, and low quality are £2.00, £1.60, and £1.20 respectively. (To simplify things we will assume that the fixed costs of operating the factory are negligible.) Another restriction is that the high quality product uses a special kind of numbering and there are only 400 sets of this available each week. The company is also in the pleasant position of being able to sell all its products, whichever it decides to make. This being the case, which products should it make if it wants to maximize profit?

We have already formulated one linear programming problem and it is not difficult to do the same for this one. Let the numbers of high, medium, and low quality products produced be x_1, x_2, and x_3 respectively.

We now aim to maximize profit $(2.0x_1 + 1.6x_2 + 1.2x_3)$ subject to the following restrictions:

on machine time $\qquad 2x_1 + x_2 + x_3 \leq 1000$ hours

on raw material availability $2x_1 + 2x_2 + x_3 \leq 1600$ pieces

on number of sets $\qquad x_1 \qquad\qquad\qquad \leq 400$ per week

If we let the profit be P, we want therefore to maximize:

$$P = 2.0x_1 + 1.6x_2 + 1.2x_3$$

subject to:

$$2x_1 + x_2 + x_3 \leq 1000$$

$$2x_1 + 2x_2 + x_3 \leq 1600$$

$$x_1 \qquad\qquad \leq 400$$

and of course:

$$x_1 \geq 0, x_2 \geq 0, x_3 \geq 0$$

If we look first at the restriction on machine time, we have $2x_1 + x_2 + x_3 \leq 1000$. If the total of hours used is less than 1000, we have some spare machine time which we will call 'slack'. At this moment we are not sure whether or not all the time will be used, so let us call this spare capacity s_1, and the restriction can be rewritten as $2x_1 + x_2 + x_3 + s_1 = 1000$. We have changed the inequality ($\leq$) to an equality ($=$) by adding the slack variable, but have not changed its meaning.

If we do the same sort of operation for the other two restrictions the disc constraint becomes $2x_1 + 2x_2 + x_3 + s_2 = 1600$ and the number of sets becomes $x_1 + s_3 = 400$. The slack variable s_2 represents unused discs and s_3 the spare number of sets. The whole problem now looks like:

$$2x_1 + x_2 + x_3 + s_1 = 1000$$

$$2x_1 + 2x_2 + x_3 + s_2 = 1600$$

$$x_1 \qquad\qquad\quad + s_3 = \quad 400$$

and we want to maximize:

$$P = 2.0x_1 + 1.6x_2 + 1.2x_3$$

We have three restrictions and six unknowns (x_1, x_2, x_3, s_1, s_2, s_3). With ordinary simultaneous equations the number of unknowns and the number of equations are the same and there is only one solution. In this case there are more unknowns than equations; therefore there are many solutions (in fact an infinite set of solutions). But we want the one that maximizes profit and are therefore interested only in the very few solutions at the boundary of the area enclosed by these equations, as explained earlier.

One solution to the equations would be $s_1 = 1000$, $s_2 = 1600$, $s_3 = 400$, $x_1 = x_2 = x_3 = 0$, and the profit $P = 0$. In other words, we do not make any profit. How does this relate to our earlier graphical solution? It can be shown that this simple solution is at one of the corners of the region – which in this case is six-dimensional. All the solutions that we will consider will be at other corners of the region. We are going to move from one corner to another getting better solutions until eventually we arrive at the best one.

Although the zero-profit solution is not of much practical use, can we improve on it? Consider, again, the profit equation $P = 2.0x_1 + 1.6x_2 + 1.2x_3$. If we look at this we see that by making any of the products we can improve the profit. So let us try to improve things by using the biggest profit improver first, that is by making some of the high quality dart boards. This will involve changing the value of x_1 from zero to some other value, and at the same time changing the values of the other variables. As things stand at present, for every high quality board made the profit will increase by £2. So why not make as many as possible – which seems sensible? A similar argument does apply to the other two products, and we could also increase our profit by making them. But, assuming that we are changing only one thing at a time, and all other things being equal, the high quality board produces the greatest marginal profit. So let us try to make some of them first.

Let us say we make $x_1 = 1$, i.e. we make one high quality dart board. The profit becomes £2 and the rest of the solution has to be made to balance. Thus s_1 now equals 998 because we have used 2 hours of machine time; $s_2 = 1598$ and $s_3 = 399$. Why not make more – increase x_1? If we make x_1 larger some of the slacks will decrease, until we get to the point where one of them becomes zero. This occurs when x_1 becomes 400, and so s_3 is zero, but $s_1 = 200$, $s_2 = 800$, and the profit P is $2 \times 400 = £800$. So we have been able to show a profit of £800. Can we do better without making any of the slack variables negative because, of course, this is not permissible. Before looking at this let us write down again our original equations:

$$2x_1 + x_2 + x_3 + s_1 = 1000 \qquad (1)$$

$$2x_1 + 2x_2 + x_3 + s_2 = 1600 \qquad (2)$$

$$x_1 \qquad\qquad\qquad + s_3 = 400 \qquad (3)$$

$$(P - 2.0x_1 - 1.6x_2 - 1.2x_3 = 0 \qquad (4)$$

Note that we have slightly transferred the profit equation to put all the x_1, x_2, and x_3 terms on the same side as in the other equations.

We have also numbered the equations to help us keep track of what we are doing. For our calculations there is a neat way of keeping account of where we are. We now want x_1 to take the value 400. So let us keep x_1 in only one equation and eliminate it from the rest, treating the series of equations as simultaneous equations. We have already found that to make $x_1 = 400$ we have to make $s_3 = 0$, so let us keep that equation, i.e. Equation (3), as it is and let us change the rest. If we want to eliminate x_1 from Equation (1) we have to multiply Equation (3) by 2 and take the whole lot from Equation (1), which results in:

$$\text{Eq. } 1 \times \quad 2x_1 + x_2 + x_3 + s_1 \qquad = 1000$$

$$\underline{- 2 \times (\text{Eq. } 2) \quad 2x_1 \qquad\qquad\qquad + 2s_3 = 800}$$
$$\qquad\qquad\qquad\qquad x_2 + x_3 + s_1 - 2s_3 = 200$$

Performing similar operations on the other equation leaves us with the following new forms of the equations:

$$(1) \qquad\quad x_2 + \quad x_3 + s_1 \qquad - 2s_3 = 200$$

$$(2) \qquad\quad 2x_2 + \quad x_3 \qquad + s_2 - 2s_3 = 800$$

$$(3) \quad x_1 \qquad\qquad\qquad\qquad\quad + s_3 = 400$$

$$(4) \ P \quad - 1.6x_2 - 1.2x_3 \qquad\quad + 2s_3 = \boxed{800}$$

At this point in the calculation the solution is:

$$x_1 = 400 \qquad\qquad s_1 = 200$$

$$x_2 = 0 \qquad\qquad s_2 = 800$$

$$x_3 = 0 \qquad\qquad s_3 = 0 \qquad\qquad P = \boxed{\text{£800}}$$

For convenience the profit figure at the lower right-hand side is enclosed in a box. Can we improve on this solution? Using reasoning similar to that used previously, the profit can be increased by now making some of the medium quality and low quality boards, i.e. by increasing x_2 or x_3. Note that we cannot increase x_1 further because that would make s_3 negative. As before, let us choose the largest, i.e. x_2 which has a value 1.6. We now have to find which of the variables x_1, s_1, and s_2 first becomes zero as x_2 is increased. In this case we see from Equation (1) that s_1 becomes zero first when x_2 takes the value 200 because x_3 and s_3 are also zero. All we have to do now is to use the equations again like simultaneous equations as we did previously but this time eliminating x_2 from all except Equation (1), and an improved solution is obtained.

The new equations are:

$$(1) \qquad x_2 + x_3 + s_1 \qquad - 2s_3 = 200$$

$$(2) \qquad\qquad - x_3 - 2s_1 + s_2 + 2s_3 = 400$$

$$(3) \qquad x_1 \qquad\qquad\qquad + s_3 = 400$$

$$(4) \ P \qquad + 0.4x_3 + 1.6s_1 \qquad - 1.2s_3 = \boxed{1120}$$

We have now increased the profit to 1120 by making $400x_1$ and $200x_2$, i.e. $400 \times £2 + 200 \times £1.6$. Can we do better?

We have not yet considered x_3 but can see from Equation (2) that if we now made s_2 zero x_3 would be $- 400$! Also with $x_1 = 400$ and $x_2 = 200$ we have already satisfied one of our original equations, Equation (1), where $2x_1 + x_2 + x_3 + s_1 = 1000$ because $2 \times 400 + 200 = 1000$.

Are we now at the end of the line? We are not, because there is still a negative term in the profit equation, Equation (4) above, where:

$$P + 0.4x_3 + 1.6s_1 - 1.2s_3 = 1120$$

We can therefore still increase profit by increasing s_3 away from zero. From Equation (2) we see that we can increase s_3 to 200 (because every other term is zero) and so our next step is to eliminate s_3 from all except Equation (2). This leads to the following set:

$$x_2 \quad - \quad s_1 + \quad s_2 \quad = \quad 600 \qquad (1)$$

$$-\,0.5x_3 - \quad s_1 + 0.5s_2 + s_3 = \quad 200 \qquad (2)$$

$$x_1 \quad +\,0.5x_3 + \quad s_1 - 0.5s_2 \quad = \quad 200 \qquad (3)$$

$$P \quad -\,0.2x_3 + 0.4s_1 + 0.6s_2 \quad = \boxed{1360} \qquad (4)$$

x_2 is now 600 and x_1 is 200 so the profit is $200 \times £2 + 600 \times £1.6 = £1360$.

We are not yet there because from Equation (4) we can increase profit yet again by increasing x_3 which we can now do because by increasing s_3 we reduced x_1. By inspection of Equation (3) we can increase x_3 to 400 if we reduce x_1 to zero, and by eliminating x_3 from Equations (2) and (4) we get:

$$x_2 \quad - \quad s_1 + \quad s_2 \quad = \quad 600 \qquad (1)$$

$$x_1 \qquad\qquad + s_3 = \quad 400 \qquad (2)$$

$$2x_1 \quad + x_3 + \quad 2s_1 - \quad s_2 \quad = \quad 400 \qquad (3)$$

$$P + 0.4x_1 \qquad\qquad + 0.8s_1 + 0.4s_2 \quad = \boxed{1440} \qquad (4)$$

This is an optimum solution because there are now no negative terms in the profit Equation (4). The best solution to the problem is therefore $x_1 = 0$, $x_2 = 600$, $x_3 = 400$, $s_1, s_2 = 0$, $s_3 = 400$, and the profit is $600 \times £1.6 + 400 \times £1.2 = £1440$. In terms of our original problem this says that we should make no high quality items, 600 medium quality, and 400 low quality dart boards, the total profit being £1440. Also, because s_1 and s_2 are zero valued we have no slack on these constraints and are using all the machine time and raw material that are available.

We seem to have a paradox in that our apparently most profitable product is not chosen. How can that come about? The reason is relatively simple. Profitability is the difference between unit selling price and unit production cost. Hence for every high quality board this is £2.00. But for every one we produce we use proportionately more capacity (machine discs, and number sets) than for any other product. The lowest quality product uses only half of the capacity per item but marginal profit is more than half of £2.00. It is £1.20 and therefore it is worth more to produce the lower quality because of the number we are able to produce.

This simple point illustrates clearly one of the main benefits of using models. They often give answers that seem unusual and need further systematic study. In this case for example we may feel that to reduce our product range (by not producing the high quality board) would be a marketing disaster. The other value of the model is that it provides guidance as to a possible solution. The economic information provided by the model is very difficult if not impossible to obtain by traditional means, and can be a very valuable aid to management decision-making.

We therefore look at the coefficients for the slack variables s_1 and s_2 which are £0.8 and £0.4 respectively. They are in fact the marginal increases in profit per unit increase in capacity respectively, and give some indication of the most costly bottlenecks. But they must be used with care; one cannot increase capacity very much before the potential benefit drops sharply. Like most aids they are of great value if used with understanding, but can often produce unwanted results if used rashly.

The final equation gives us useful financial information for this purpose:

$$P + 0.4x_1 + 0.8s_1 + 0.4s_2 = £1440$$

One interpretation of $0.4x_1$ in the equation is that if we manufactured x_1 then we will make 40 pence less profit for every one produced. This suggests that before it is worth making the high quality product we have to increase the marginal profit by at least 40 pence, by increasing the selling price, by decreasing production costs, or by some combination of these. For example, if we could get an extra 50 pence for each item the new coefficient for x_1 would be $40 - 50 = -£0.10$; the profit equation would then become $P - 0.1x_1 + 0.8s_1 + 0.4s_2$, and the solution would no longer be optimal. Another iteration would be necessary which would ensure that some of the high quality product would be made.

Using the computer

We have looked at some simple examples illustrating the use of linear programming, and we have performed a bit of elementary arithmetic. The numbers used so far were all chosen for ease of calculation and were representative rather than real.

In real situations the number of equations and the decimal nature of many of the digits involved make the method of simultaneous equations we have described too laborious and difficult. Computer programmes have been written for many linear programming problems, and it is worth taking a little time to illustrate the computer method of solution, because it will also help the reader learn how to solve simple linear programming for himself by a rather neater technique than that we have described although it still uses the same basic logic.

This method is known as the Simplex method because the kind of geometrical diagram shown in Fig. 7.4 is known as a Simplex. The rules and problem calculations are shown in Tables 7.1 and 7.2 respectively. The variables which are in solution are known as basic variables and are given in the left-hand column. Their values are read off on the right-hand side. Other variables having zero value are written along the top of each tableau. The rules may seem strange but are very easy to operate. Tableau A contains exactly the same information as the initial equations when fully written out (see Table 7.2).

Table 7.1. Operating rules for Simplex method.

---

(1) Find an initial basic feasible solution.
(2) Check the tableau for optimality. If all the objective row has positive entries the optimum has been reached.
(3) If not optimum, find the largest negative in the objective row. This gives us the 'entering variable' and its column.
(4) For all 'positive elements' in the entering variable column, calculate θ, i.e. value in right-hand side divided by value in entering variable column. The minimum of these θ values gives the 'departing variable' row. Where the 'entering variable' column and 'departing variable' row intersect is termed the 'pivot element'.
(5) Make a new tableau, interchanging the departing and entering variables.
(6) Update the coefficients in the tableau by the following rules:
     (i) pivot– invert
     (ii) pivot column– divide by pivot and change sign
     (iii) pivot row– divide by pivot
     (iv) all other coefficients:

$$\text{new value} = \text{old value} - \frac{\left(\begin{array}{c}\text{coefficient in same}\\\text{row but pivot column}\end{array}\right) \times \left(\begin{array}{c}\text{coefficient in same}\\\text{column but pivot row}\end{array}\right)}{\text{pivot}}$$

(7) Go back to (2)

Tableau A is seen to have the same form as the first set of equations on page 113 except that the order is different because the slack variables, being initially non-zero, are now on the left-hand side (LHS). This is, of course, the initial basic solution (step 1 of Table 7.1) where x_1, x_2, and x_3 are all zero and the profit is also zero. This is clearly not an optimum solution (step 2 of Table 7.1) because the objective row (which indicates the profit) has all negative coefficients. The largest negative in this row is -2 (step 3 of Table 7.1). The entering variable for the next tableau is thus x_1. The departing one is s_3 because 400 is the lowest value in the right-hand side after dividing by the appropriate coefficient in the x_1 column (step 4 of Table 7.1).

We thus interchange x_1 and s_3 and make a new tableau B (step 5). The new coefficients are obtained as follows:

The pivot coefficient at the new x_1, s_3 intersection is the inverse of the previous coefficient at the old intersection. Since this was 1, the inverse is also 1. (Later in Tableau D we see coefficients of $\frac{1}{2}$, the inverse of 2.)

Table 7.2. Calculations using Simplex method.

	Pivot element	LHS	x_1	x_2	x_3	RHS	θ
				Non-basic variables			
Tableau A	Basic variables	s_1	2	1	1	1000	$1000/2 = 500$
		s_2	2	2	1	1600	$1600/2 = 800$
		s_3	①	0	0	400	$400/1 = 400*$min → Departing variable
	objective	P	—2	—1.6	—1.2	⬚0	—Current solution value
			↑ Entering variable				

			s_3	x_2	x_3	RHS	θ
Tableau B		s_1	—2	①	1	200	$200/1 = 200*$min → Departing variable
		s_2	—2	2	1	800	$800/2 = 400$
		x_1	1	0	0	400	$400/0 = \infty$
		P	2	—1.6	—1.2	⬚800	
				↑			

			s_3	s_1	x_3	RHS	θ
Tableau C		x_2	—2	1	1	200	not allowed
		s_2	②	—2	—1	400	$400/2 = 200*$min → Departing variable
		x_1	1	0	0	400	$400/1 = 400$
		P	—1.2	1.6	0.4	⬚1120	
			↑				

			s_2	s_1	x_3	RHS	θ
Tableau D		x_2	1	—1	0	600	$600/0 = \infty$
		s_3	$\frac{1}{2}$	—1	—$\frac{1}{2}$	200	not allowed
		x_1	—$\frac{1}{2}$	1	②$\frac{1}{2}$	200	$200/\frac{1}{2} = 400*$min → Departing variable
		P	0.6	0.4	—0.2	⬚1360	
					↑		

			s_2	s_1	x_1	RHS
Tableau E		x_2	1	—1	0	600
		s_3	0	0	1	400
		x_3	—1	2	2	400
		P	0.4	0.8	0.4	⬚1440

Down the remainder of the pivot column, the s_3 column in Tableau B, the new coefficients are the old ones divided by the previous pivot coefficient, with the sign changed.

Hence, at the intersection of s_3 and s_1, the coefficient changes from $+2$ to $-2/1 = -2$. At s_3, s_2 the coefficient is also $-2/1 = -2$. In the pivot row, i.e. the new x_1 row in Tableau B, the old coefficients are just divided by the old pivot coefficient without a change of sign.

The other coefficients are changed by the seemingly complex rule:

new value $=$ old value$-$

$$\frac{\left(\begin{array}{c}\text{coefficient in same row}\\ \text{but pivot column}\end{array}\right) \times \left(\begin{array}{c}\text{coefficient in same column}\\ \text{but pivot row}\end{array}\right)}{\text{pivot}}$$

As an example, take the intersection of x_2 and s_2. The old coefficient here, from Tableau A, was 2. The coefficient in the same row but pivot column is at the intersection of s_3 and s_2; this is 2. The coefficient in the same but pivot row is at the intersection of x_2 and x_1; this is zero. The pivot coefficient is, of course, 1. Thus, the new value at this intersection is:

$$2 - (2 \times 0)/1 = 2$$

We leave it to the reader to decide whether he wishes to complete Tableau B and proceed now to the others to the same optimum solution as before.

In practice O.R. workers almost always nowadays would use a computer to perform all the calculations, and the preceding few pages have been written to provide insights as well as to teach the method. Most (if not all) computers today have packaged computer programmes that will solve linear programming problems. All we have to do is to get the data into a form that the computer will understand. As stated previously, the hard part is in formulating the problem, i.e. getting it into its mathematical form. Once this has been done the computer takes over the laborious calculations.

If the problem is to be repeatedly solved using updated information, it may pay us to write two other programmes ourselves as shown diagrammatically in Fig. 7.5. These are known as the 'matrix generator' and 'report writer' respectively, and the three programmes can be coupled internally in the computer without having printing documents or cards in between.

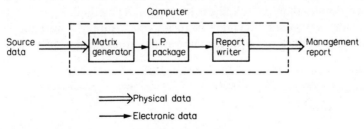

Fig. 7.5. Schematic representation of set of programmes.

The matrix generator saves manual calculations before getting the linear programme solved. It is not by sheer chance that the development and use of linear programming models has been parallel to that of computers.

Without the computer we could not solve most of the problems we have today.

What size of problem will computers solve? The answer is 'almost unlimited'. For example, one of the largest problems to be solved in Europe by a major oil company has about 6000 constraints and about 10000 variables. This is about the limit of most large computers at the time of writing but no doubt it will be surpassed. One problem with such large models is the handling of vast amounts of input and output information. It could be that the limit will be the human capacity to cope with such a complexity rather than lack of computer ability.

In process industries, where the technology of the production process is very well understood, linear programming has proved a boon. Some companies have even set up linear programming departments which deal with large complex models that use up a lot of computer time. The savings can be enormous; even a few per cent on hundreds of millions of pounds is a lot of money. Most customers of the Readers Digest have been the subject of a linear programme model of their consumer tastes!

However, in most situations the 'typical' model (if there is such a thing) is much smaller with from ten to a few hundred constraints and variables. Such models take little computer time and cost only a few pounds to solve on today's computers. The cost element that we now have to watch and control is the collection and analysis of data before using the linear programming package.

Other programming methods

Some problems have special features which make them easier to solve. For example, the problem of which goods to send from which warehouse to which customer can often be an example of the 'transportation problem' of linear programming. In such cases the routine for solving the problem is much simpler than the full linear programming method.

Consider a company having 3 factories which supply 4 warehouses with the items (machines) it requires. The various stocks and requirements are:

Factory	Machines	Warehouse	Requirement
A	6	1	3
B	6	2	7
C	5	3	3
		4	4
Total	17	Total	17

Transportation costs vary with the initial location and final destination, and are given in the following matrix:

	Warehouse 1	2	3	4
A	6	7	8	5
Factory B	8	5	6	5
C	9	8	6	8

Our problem is to allocate the goods in a way that gives the least total transportation cost.

The method of solution has similarities to that of linear programming, being an iterative method, finding better and better solutions. We will show the workings of the procedure without proof. First of all we need a feasible solution. This can be obtained by inspecting the cost matrix and making an arbitrary allocation. An easier method is to use what is known as the North-West-corner rule. Starting in the top left-hand corner, allocate as many machines as possible. It is 3 in this case because that is the maximum required by Warehouse 1. This leaves 3 still at Factory A, so we try to allocate these to the next warehouse. Allocating 3 to Warehouse 2 uses up all the surplus at Factory A, so we now move on to Factory B, etc. Continuing in this fashion always gives us a feasible allocation. (If there are more available than required, or vice versa, all we have to do is put in a zero-cost dummy warehouse or factory to mop up the slack.) The initial allocation is:

	Warehouse 1	2	3	4	Available
A	3	3			6
Factory B		4	2		6
C			1	4	5
Required	3	7	3	4	

at a cost of:

$$(3 \times 6) + (3 \times 7) + (4 \times 5) + (2 \times 6) + (1 \times 6) + (3 \times 8) = £101$$

We now have to look for lower cost solutions. This is done by allocating a series of 'shadow costs' to the factories and warehouses. They may be thought of as a cost of dispatch from each factory and a cost of reception at each warehouse. The first shadow cost can be chosen arbitrarily (say 0), and the rest have then to be chosen such that for allocated cells the sum of the two corresponding costs must be equal to the unit cost of that cell (C_{ij} say). Let us call the dispatch costs U_i, and the reception costs V_j, and their sum $\bar{C}_{ij} = U_i + V_j$. Our restriction is then that for allocated cells $C_{ij} = \bar{C}_{ij}$. For example, let $U_1 = 0$, i.e. put the cost of despatch from Factory A to be 0. We have an allocation in the Factory A Warehouse 1 cell, and therefore we must have $U_1 + V_1 = C_{11} = 6$. This gives $V_1 = 6$. Also we have an allocation in the A2 cell; therefore $U_1 + V_2 = C_{12} = 7 = 0 + V_2$, i.e. $V_2 = 7$. Continuing in this fashion we find the following shadow costs:

	1	2	3	4	U_i
A	6	7	C_{13}	C_{14}	0
B	C_{21}	5	6	C_{24}	-2
C	C_{31}	C_{32}	6	8	-2
V_j	6	7	8	10	

The actual numbers depend on the initial arbitrary allocation, but their relative magnitudes depend on the transportation cost matrix.

What do we do with these shadow costs? For all unallocated cells we work out the sum of the shadow costs ($\bar{C}_{ij} = U_i + V_j$), e.g. $\bar{C}_{21} = U_2 + V_1 = -2 + 6 = 4$. Then we compare this with the true costs, i.e. work out $C_{ij} - \bar{C}_{ij}$. It can be shown that if this is negative for any cell the optimum solution has not been reached, and allocation in the cell in question will improve the solution. The difference between the two costs gives the decrease in cost that is brought about by unit allocation in that cell. Let us try it out on our problem using one matrix for the calculations, with each cell having three numbers:

If we do this for our problem we get:

	1	2	3	4	U_i
A			[8] [8][5]	[10]	0
			0	-5	
B	[8] [4]			[5] [8]	-2
	4			-3	
C	[9] [4][8]	[5]			-2
	5	3			
V_j	6	7	7	10	

As an example take the B4 cell: $\bar{C}_{ij} = -2 + 10 = 8$, $C_{ij} = 5$, hence $C_{ij} - \bar{C}_{ij} = -3$. There are negative values in some of the cells, so we have not yet found the optimum solution. The A4 cell gives the largest cost difference (-5); therefore let us allocate as many as possible into this cell, say x. If we do this the other allocations have to be adjusted to make the matrix balance; we get:

3	3-x		x
	4-x	2-x	
		1-x	4-x

and the maximum value that x can take is 2. Putting 2 into this cell, we get the improved allocation:

3	1		2
	6		
		3	2

at a cost of $£101 - (2 \times 5) = £91$.

The whole analysis is now repeated to see if we have reached the optimum. First of all we have to find new shadow costs, starting with an initial arbitrary allocation. Let U_1 be 0 once again; doing this we get:

U_i

6	7		5	0
	5			-2
		6	8	3

V_j 6   7   3   5

The $C_{ij} - \bar{C}_{ij}$ matrix now becomes:

		[8] 5	[3]	0
[8] 4	[4]	[6] 5	[1][5] 2	[3] -2
[9] 0	[9][8] -2	[10]		3

6   7   3   5

and the maximum we can allocate in C2 (the only negative cell) is:

3	1-x		2+x
	6		
	x	3	2-x

The new allocation is:

3			3
	6		
	1	3	1

at a cost of $91 - (1 \times 2) = £89$.

Performing our analysis again we now get:

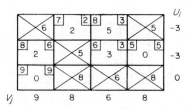

All the calculations have been done on the same matrix, and from the calculations we can see that there are no more negative cells. Hence our previous solution is optimal, and is:

 Factory A supplies 3 to warehouse 1, and 3 to warehouse 4

 Factory B supplies 6 to warehouse 2

 Factory C supplies 1 to warehouse 2, 3 to warehouse 3, and 1 to warehouse 4,

the total cost of transportation being £89.

From our last matrix we see that certain cells have $C_{ij} - \bar{C}_{ij} = 0$. This means that other minimum cost allocations are possible, i.e. alternative optima exist. We will leave these for the interested reader to try and find.

We can sometimes come up against problems that are much more difficult to solve than linear programming problems. One such case occurs if we need whole-number solutions, and such problems are known as integer programming problems. Such problems are of the selection/rejection type where you either select or reject and it is not possible to choose a value of, say, 0.3. Examples that we may easily understand are those involving the number of tankers necessary for some sort of transportation, the building and location of a number of depots, and the decision to produce a few large manufactured items. In other words, what use is 0.7 of a ship? Another example of its use is given be Elson with regard to the problem of siting warehouses.

It is much more difficult to solve these sorts of problems in the sense that they cost a great deal more to solve. The space and time used inside a computer are considerably increased. Although packages are available that will solve many problems, and this does not present difficulties, the cost may be very large, and hence the cost of errors in data, incorrect model, etc. correspondingly increased. If possible it is best to get some expert advice before using integer programming packages. But the future looks a little brighter with the falling of computing costs in general. It may well be that in a few years time integer programming could be as readily and cheaply available as linear programming is today.

There are also many other programming methods that have been produced but which are still a long way from complete commercial viability. One problem which may arise in practice is that the relationship may be non-linear. A common occurrence of this type is in the profit/cost equation where we often get economies of scale. In linear programming if an item costs £10 then for ten items it costs £100, and for one hundred it is assumed to cost £1000. But in many practical situations it is more than likely that this latter figure is too high, i.e. discounts often apply for large quantities. Many attempts have been made to derive mathematical routines that will solve such problems, and they are usually called 'non-linear programming' methods, but they have achieved little success so far. In practice in such situations one may often overcome such difficulties by making linear approximations. One fairly successful method of doing this has been developed called 'separable programming' which is now commercially available.

Another difficulty that has been investigated is the problem of uncertainty, i.e. when some of the numerical information cannot be predicted with complete confidence. Again various techniques such as 'chance-constrained programming' and 'stochastic programming' have been and are being developed, and they offer promise for the future.

Finally, another technique that is often mentioned is 'dynamic programming'. This is in essence somewhat different from the other programming methods and is a way of looking at multi-stage decision problems. It can become very complex mathematically but is also very powerful. In chapter 9 we consider the problem of how to make decisions and we introduce the technique of decision trees. Dynamic programming is a technique for tackling similar sorts of situations but working in much more detail. For anyone interested the book by Houlden gives a very useful introduction.

REFERENCES

Elson, D.G., 'Site location via mixed-integer programming,' *O.R.Q.,* Vol. 23, No. 1, March 1972, pp. 31–44.
Houlden, B.T., *Operational Research Techniques*,
Lockett, A.G., 'A model of the hide-leather sequence in a tannery,' *O.R.Q.,* Vol. 24, No. 4, December 1973, pp. 491–501.

BIBLIOGRAPHY

Beale, E.M.L., *Mathematical Programming in Practice*, Pitman, London, 1968.

Hadley, G., *Linear Programming*, Addison Wesley, Reading, Mass., 1965.

Henderson, A. and Schlaifer, R., 'Mathematical programming, better information for better decision-making,' *H.B.R.,* Vol. 32, No. 3, May-June 1954.

Jones, W.G. and Rope, C.M., 'Linear programming applied to production planning: a case study,' *O.R.Q.*, Vol. 15, No. 4, December 1964, pp. 293–302.

Lockett, A.G., *Resource Allocation for Management*, Gowes, London, 1976.

Nicholson, T.A.J. and Pullen, R.D., 'Dynamic programming applied to ship fleet management,' *O.R.Q.*, Vol. 22, No. 3, September 1971, pp. 211–220.

Pengilly, P.J. and Moss, A.J., 'Choice of a new product, its selling pattern and price,' *O.R.Q.*, Vol. 20, No. 2, June 1969, pp. 174–185.

Rothstein, M., 'Scheduling manpower by mathematical programming,' *Industrial Engineering*, Vol. 4, No. 4, April 1972, pp. 29–33.

Russell, E., 'Lessons in structuring large LP models,' *Industrial Engineering*, Vol. 2, No. 9, March 1970, pp. 12–18.

Sasieni, M.W., Yaspan, A. and Friedman, L., *Operations Research: Methods and Problems*, Wiley, New York, 1959.

Tillman, F.A. and Lee, E.S., 'On-line blending for production profit,' *Control Engineering*, Vol 15, No. 10, October 1968, pp. 111–115.

8 Planning Projects

To every man there openeth
A way, and ways, and a way,
And the high soul climbs the high way,
And the low soul gropes the low;
And in between on the misty flats,
The rest drift to and fro;
But to every man there openeth
A high way and a low,
And every man decideth
The way his soul shall go.

John Oxenham, A High Way and a Low

The main lesson of the preceding two chapters on production control and resource allocation is that information is essential for control purposes. The more the information the better the control. This is one of the great principles of Operational Research and it has been the stimulus behind the development of network analysis for planning and scheduling. The use of this technique has expanded substantially in the past few years and it is now one of the most powerful means of controlling complex scheduling operations such as the building of a new factory, the maintenance programme of complex plant, and the marketing of new products.

The scheduling problems appropriate for network analysis are different from those considered earlier on pages 99, 105, and 120. On these earlier pages the optimum use of available resources for scheduling continuous and largely repetitive operations was considered. In network analysis the deployment of available resources for the completion of a non-repetitive task within the minimum time or for the minimum cost is studied. As the use and experience of network analysis grows, and the scope of linear programming widens, the distinction between these two types of scheduling becomes blurred, but at present they are still fairly clear-cut.

A simple illustration of the purpose of network analysis can be given in the following way. Every morning, say, you toast three pieces of toast on a grill which will take two pieces of bread at a time. (Although, you may argue, this is a repetitive task it is not a continuously repetitive one in the assembly line sense and hence it is appropriate for consideration by network analysis and not linear programming.) The schedule for the operation may be as follows:

Toast one side of pieces A and B	30 sec
Toast other side of pieces A and B	30 sec
Toast one side of piece C	30 sec
Toast other side of piece C	30 sec
Total time	120 sec

The whole schedule could be shortened if, as shown in a famous wartime advertisement for fuel saving, the toasting sequence were as follows:

Toast one side of pieces A and B	30 sec
Toast one side of C and other side of A	30 sec
Toast other side of B and C	30 sec
Total time	90 sec

Although this is a very trivial example of how time can be saved by optimizing the logical sequence of events, many similar opportunities occur in large-scale development and maintenance programmes and can be overlooked but for the rigorous discipline imposed by network analysis.

A slightly more complex example, involving multi-activity analysis, could follow the toasting sequence when you get out your car and drive to work. The schedule for the operation may be:

Walk to garage doors	10 sec
Open garage doors	5 sec
Walk to car	5 sec
Enter and start car	10 sec
Drive car out of garage	5 sec
Walk back to garage	5 sec
Shut garage doors	5 sec
Walk back to car and drive off	10 sec
Total time	55 sec

Now, if you were desperately short of time you would ask your wife to open the garage doors and the schedule would then be (time in seconds):

Your wife		You	
Walk to garage doors	10	Walk to car by back door of garage	10
Open garage doors	5	Enter and start car	5
Wait	5	Drive car out of garage	5

The total time you have spent is reduced to 20 seconds and hence there is a saving to you of 35 seconds. If your wife were to close the garage doors and join you in the car only a further 15 seconds would have been taken, still leaving a saving of 20 seconds. The total time spent by you and your wife in the whole operation is still only 55 seconds and it thus has, in total, been no more costly in time despite the overall saving of 20 seconds. It is this kind of planning, together with that shown in the first example, which, on a vastly larger scale, is reported to have cut the completion time of the Polaris missile system from seven to five years, and reduced unproductive time on maintenance shut-down in chemical works.

Network based techniques are extensively applied to operations such as: construction and building projects; maintenance and periodic shut-down of plant; new product launch; applied research and development work; complex administrative procedures and routines.

A number of alternative versions of network analysis exist:

Critical Path Method (CPM)

Critical Path Scheduling (CPS)

Programme Evaluation and Review Technique (PERT).

All the techniques are essentially the same, and historical backgrounds can be found in Lockyer.

Network analysis may be applied to a project (or operation) with the following characteristics:

(a) The project can be broken down into a number of separate activities (or tasks).
(b) The time required (duration) of each activity can be estimated.
(c) To complete the project certain activities must precede others, while some activities may be carried out in parallel.
(d) Each activity requires some combination of resources in terms of men of various skills, facilities, materials, or money. There may be more than one feasible combination of resources for an activity, and each combination is likely to result in a different estimate of activity duration.

Because network planning is one of the most used techniques in practice, we give a fairly comprehensive description in what follows.

Construction of Networks

The project is represented graphically by a diagram consisting of two building blocks: lines to represent activities; and circles, known as events, to represent points in time. An activity consumes time and/or resources, while an event is a stage in the life of the project when defined preceding activities will all have been completed and succeeding activities can start.

All activities and events associated with the project are joined together to form a single network which illustrates the logical sequence of activities and events.

An example network is shown in Fig. 8.1. In this case 6 activities, labelled A to G, are involved. A short description is attached to each activity in

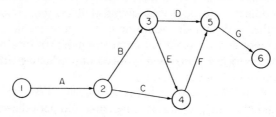

Fig. 8.1.

practice. The usual convention is to treat time as increasing from left to right, and to attach a number to each node (event) as shown. Thus activity C, for example, is uniquely defined by its preceding and succeeding event numbers as activity 2–4.

The above network embodies the following relationships:
  (i) Event 1 is the starting point of the project.
 (ii) Activities B and C cannot start until A is completed.
(iii) Activities D and E cannot start until B is completed.
(iv) Activity F cannot start until E and C are completed.
 (v) Activity G cannot start until D and F are completed.
(vi) Event 6 is the end of the project.

There are a number of rules to observe when constructing a network, included here for completeness.

Rule 1. No activity may be allowed to 'dangle'. For example, activity 2–3

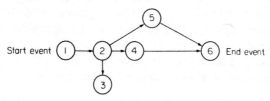

Fig. 8.2.

has no connection with the end event. The network must be modified to bring activity 2–3 into a path which leads to the end event, perhaps by connecting 3 directly to 6 with an activity which does not consume time or resources. Such an activity is known as a 'dummy'.

Rule 2. Closed loops are not allowed. For example, the 'loop' shown in Fig. 8.3 represents a cyclical relationship between the activities.

Fig. 8.3.,

Rule 3. Parallel activities cannot have both the same start and end events, since this leads to confusion of identity. This is overcome by inserting a dummy activity which has zero duration and uses no resources. For example, Fig. 8.4 is redrawn as Fig. 8.5. It is usual to represent the dummy, C, by a broken line.

Fig. 8.4.,

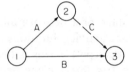

Fig. 8.5.,

Rule 4. No event can have two or more preceding activities and two or more succeeding unless *all* the succeeding activities cannot start until all the preceding activities are completed. For example, the network in Fig. 8.6 means that: (i) activity 3–5 may not start until both activities 1–3 and 2–3 are complete; (ii) activity 3–4 may not start until both activities 1–3 and 2–3 are complete. If the commencement of activity 3–5 depends on the completion of activity 2–3 and not on the completion of activity 1–3 as well, then an additional event (6) and a dummy activity (3–6) are required as shown in Fig. 8.7.

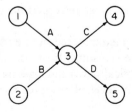

Fig. 8.6.

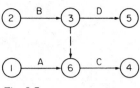

Fig. 8.7.

All that is needed to draw a network is some large sheet of paper, a pencil, and a rubber. In a large network of more than fifty or so activities several attempts may be necessary before the inter-relationships are satisfactorily included.

Analysis of networks

Aspects of the analysis which are of major importance are time analysis and resource analysis.

Time analysis

This is normally the first stage of a network analysis, and involves a consideration of the estimates of activity durations only. Of particular interest is the deduction of the 'critical path'. This is defined as that unbroken sequence of events and activities through the network from the first to the last event which add up to a total duration that is greater than that along any other path. This duration then equals the duration of the project, provided that scarcity of a resource does not constitute a bottleneck at any stage, and provided that there are no uncertain activity durations.

Resource analysis

It is often necessary to supplement a time analysis with a resource allocation technique. The simplest resource analysis simply provides an aggregated picture of each of the resources required during the project's life as a result of the time analysis, assuming, for example, that all activities are scheduled at their earliest possible start times. More sophisticated procedures reschedule activities in order to achieve certain objectives. Some common objectives are:
1. To contain overall resource requirements within prescribed limits over the project's life. This may mean that the project duration set by the time analysis (critical path) can no longer be met.
2. To maintain a steady level of resource usage over all or part of the project's life.
3. To build up or run down resource usage in some prescribed manner.

Complex problems can arise at this stage: the interchange ability of resources, particularly manpower; the trade-off between resource scheduling objectives and project duration; the extent to which additional resources can be made available and at what cost; idle resources; the maintenance of flexibility in the selected schedule to cope with the unexpected; the cost of a project over-running its planned completion date; and many more.

An example analysis

Time and resource analysis are explained with the aid of the example network shown in Fig. 8.8. On each activity the first number represents the duration

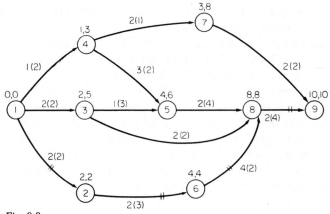

Fig. 8.8.

in weeks while the bracketed number represents the number of men required. We assume that one type of skilled manpower is the only scarce resource. The nodes have simply been numbered from 1 to 9 in an arbitrary fashion.

Time analysis of Fig. 8.8

The earliest start times of each event in the network are first deduced. This is the first of the pair of numbers shown above each event. In a network of up to about 200 activities this is easily done on the network diagram itself. For large projects standard packages are available with most computers.

The start time of event 1 is set at zero, and the start times of adjacent events are determined by addition of activity times, working through the network until the end event is reached. For example, the earliest time of reaching event 4 is in 1 week, and of event 3 is 2 weeks.

In order to achieve event 5 activities 4–5 *and* 3–5 must be completed. The earliest time of completing 4–5 is $1 + 3 = 4$ weeks, and of 3–5 is $2 + 1 = 3$

weeks. Thus the earliest time of reaching event 5 is the greater of these, i.e. 4 weeks, and this is entered above the node.

Proceeding in this way sequentially through the network the end event will eventually be reached. The earliest time of the end event is the shortest time required to complete the project as planned. In the example this is 10 weeks. By noting the activity times which were added together during the calculation of this critical time, the 'critical activities' can immediately be deduced. In the example these are: 1–2, 2–6, 6–8, 8–9 (i.e. $2 + 2 + 4 + 2 = 10$ weeks). The critical activities are often indicated with a double bar, as shown in Fig. 8.8 and this sequence of activities is known as the 'critical path'.

It is sometimes useful to calculate the latest start times of each event in the network if the critical time is not to be exceeded. The calculation proceeds from the end event, working back towards the start event. The latest time of the end event is set equal to the critical time of the project, 10 weeks in the example. It is then necessary to work backwards through the project, subtracting activity times. Thus the latest time to event 7 is $10 - 2 = 8$ weeks, and to event 8 is also $10 - 2 = 8$ weeks.

Node 4 is connected to nodes 5 and 7. By route 4–7 the latest time to node 4 is $8 - 2 = 6$ weeks; by route 4–5 the latest time to node 4 is $6 - 3 = 3$ weeks. Clearly node 4 must be reached after 3 weeks at the latest if the project is not to be delayed. Thus the latest time to node 4 is 3 weeks, and this is entered on the diagram. Working backwards in this way the start event will be finally reached. The latest time for the start event must of course be zero, and this provides a check on the calculations.

Non-critical elements

Activities and events not on the critical path are less important to the timely completion of the project. However, if there is a limit to the amount of spare time, and if deviations to plan occur, the critical path may switch to a new route, delaying project completion.

The slack associated with each event may be calculated as the difference between the latest and earliest times at each node, and this gives a measure of the 'criticality' of each event. Events on the critical path have zero slack. These may be set out as shown in Table 8.1 for the example project.

From Table 8.1 events 4 and 5 have the smallest slack apart from the critical events. Thus activities 1–4 and 4–5 should be reviewed as well as the critical activities, if there is reason to believe that the activity durations of 1 and 3 weeks may be on the optimistic side.

An analysis of the 'floating' time available to each activity may also be undertaken, and this is the time available to an activity in addition to its planned duration. Two types of float, one or more of which are sometimes calculated for each activity, are defined as, and calculated from:

Table 8.1.

Event	Earliest time	Latest time	Event slack
1	0	0	0
2	2	2	0
3	2	5	3
4	1	3	2
5	4	6	2
6	4	4	0
7	3	8	5
8	8	8	0
9	10	10	0

1. *Total float.* The maximum increase in activity duration which can occur without increasing the project duration.

Total float = Latest finish − Earliest start − Duration
e.g. for activity 3–5, total float = 6 − 2 − 1 = 3.

2. *Free float.* The maximum increase in activity duration which can occur without altering the floats available to subsequent activities.

Free float = Earliest time of succeeding event − Earliest time
of preceding event − duration.
e.g. for activity 3–5, free float = 4 − 2 − 1 = 1.

An analysis of the floats for each activity in the example network is given in Table 8.2. (In practice the total float, if any, is usually calculated.)

Table 8.2.

Activity	Duration	Start time Earliest	Start time Latest	Finish time Earliest	Finish time Latest	Floats Total	Floats Free
1–2	2	0	0	2	2	0	0
1–3	2	0	3	2	5	3	0
1–4	1	0	2	1	3	2	0
4–5	3	1	3	4	6	2	0
4–7	2	1	6	3	8	5	0
3–5	1	2	5	3	6	3	1
3–8	2	2	6	4	8	4	4
5–8	2	4	6	6	8	2	2
2–6	2	2	2	4	4	0	0
6–8	4	4	4	8	8	0	0
7–9	2	3	8	5	10	5	5
8–9	2	8	8	10	10	0	0

Resource analysis of Fig. 8.8

In the foregoing time analysis the utilization and availability of resources have been ignored. We have estimated that each activity in the example requires the resources shown in Table 8.3.

Table 8.3.

Activity	Duration	Manpower	Duration × manpower
1–2	2	2	4
1–3	2	2	4
1–4	1	2	2
4–7	2	1	2
4–5	3	2	6
3–5	1	3	3
3–8	2	2	4
2–6	2	3	6
7–9	2	2	4
5–8	2	4	8
8–9	2	4	8
6–8	4	2	8
			Total = 59 man-weeks

Resource Allocation

The simplest form of resource analysis is known as 'resource allocation'. For each resource type, the resources required by each activity are totalled and represented graphically over time. Earliest start times for the activities are usually assumed, and no consideration of the overall availability of resources is included.

For the example project, the accumulation for manpower is shown in the lower half of Fig. 8.9. The upper half of this figure shows a graphical construction of the network on a time scale. This is similar to the traditional Gantt chart but has the advantages of depicting sequencing restrictions (as thick vertical bars) and floats on activities (as dashed horizontal lines).

More complex forms of analysis can be used to re-schedule the activities in order to produce, for example, a more smoothed or levelled accumulation of each resource type. If the minimum project duration of 10 weeks is not to be exceeded, then some levelling may be possible by shifting the activity starts within the constraints set by the floats. In this case critical activities cannot be re-scheduled. In Fig. 8.10 is shown the result of a manual attempt to re-schedule the example project to produce a smoothed resource usage of between 5 and 7 men which is certainly an improvement on Fig. 8.9 which fluctuated between 2 and 11 men.

The schedule of Fig. 8.10 was produced by a trial and error process using Fig. 8.9 as a starting point. The floats indicated in Fig. 8.9 show the re-

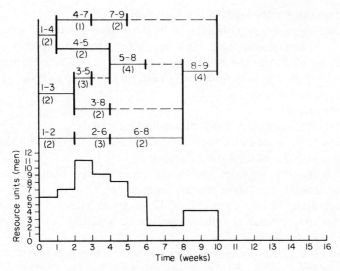

Fig. 8.9. Network constructed as a form of Gantt chart, together with a histogram of overall resource usage.

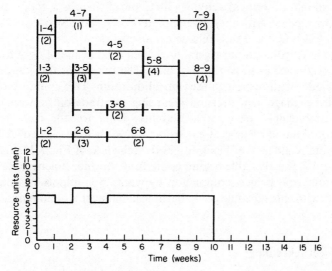

Fig. 8.10. Re-scheduled activities to produce a smoother resource usage within the critical proper duration of 10 weeks.

scheduling options. Provided that the network is not too large, say greater than 50 activities, manual scheduling by trial and error is quite feasible after a little practice, even if a number of resource types are involved. But for large networks and frequent up-dating a computer routine becomes a practical necessity if the analysis is to be timely.

The calculation of truly optimal schedules for large networks is not feasible even with the largest computer. However, several heuristic rules have been suggested which enable the computer to produce reasonably efficient schedules even in networks with thousands of activities. An example of a heuristic procedure is as follows:

Begin at time 0
(1) List all the activities that are logically free to start.
(2) Sort them in order of increasing float, and for those with the same float in order of increasing duration.
(3) Schedule the activities one by one from the list, checking resource availability, until some resource is used up.
(4) Step along in time until one of the on-going activities is completed. This may release activities which were logically held up and will release resources.
(5) Adjust the float on those activities that were logically free to start but have been held up by lack of resources.
(6) Repeat steps 1 to 5 until all activities have been scheduled.

This procedure is based on the idea that in the event of a resource bottle-neck one should do critical activities first, and if there is a choice between activities with equal criticality, one should do the shortest one, i.e. the one which will finish first and thus release resources first.

A possible schedule for a project in which a total availability of four men cannot be exceeded is shown in Fig. 8.11. The overall project duration increases by 50% with respect to the critical duration. This could become the subject of a management decision regarding the trade-off between project duration and overall resource availability. Data for the costs of additional resources and of project extension would then be needed. A further point to note is the lack of flexibility in the schedule of Fig. 8.11. Except in period 6 and 7, the available resources are fully utilized. If activity estimates are uncertain, and project completion by week 15 is important, managing the project with this schedule could become a manager's nightmare!

Multi-project scheduling

In an organization where projects are simultaneously on-going, and using a common set of limited resources, a complex resource allocation problem involving resource sharing can arise. Since the projects are competing for resources, information on desired or essential completion dates and on relative priority is required. In these situations it becomes almost essential to use a multi-project scheduling computer algorithm. Such packages are available from most of the major computer manufacturers.

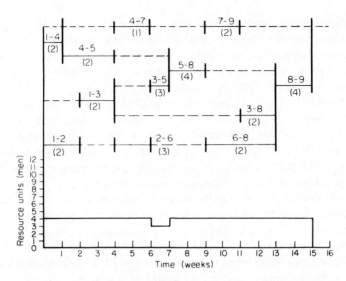

Fig. 8.11. Re-scheduled activities to produce a resource usage that does not exceed 4 men.

Precedence networks

The network notation used in this chapter so far is 'arrow diagram' notation, so called because the activities are shown as arrows. Arrow diagrams are sometimes known as *i-j* networks (because activities are defined as lying between two events, say the *i*th and the *j*th events) or as event-on-node networks.

The original CPM and PERT systems were based on arrow diagram for-mulations of the network but a different notation is now gaining ground. This is known as the 'activity-on-node' or precedence network notation and is illustrated in Fig. 8.12 which shows the same project plan as Fig. 8.8.

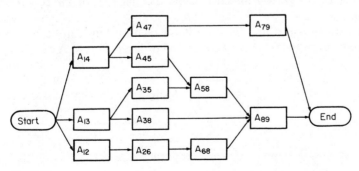

Fig. 8.12.

In this notation activities are shown in boxes. The arrows in the diagram simply show logical precedence and do not denote activities. Where two or more arrows terminate at an activity, all must be traversed before the activity may begin. Where two or more arrows leave an activity, all may be followed as soon as the activity is complete.

The concepts of critical path, float, and resource allocation are independent of the notation used, and most computer packages now permit the network to be specified in either arrow diagram or activity-on-node format.

Some people find notation of Fig. 8.12 easier to understand than that of of Fig. 8.8. No dummy activities are required in precedence networks, but it is not so convenient to draw them against a time scale.

One advantage of the activity-on-node formulation is that it permits more general dependences between the activities to be represented.

As an example, consider the case of a construction project in which a trench has to be dug and then filled with concrete. If it is a long trench it will normally be possible to begin concreting before the trench is completed, so the representation shown in Fig. 8.13 would be incorrect.

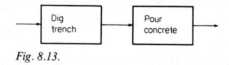

Fig. 8.13.

The traditional solution to this problem is to split the trenching activity into several stages and to show the concreting as dependent on completion of stage 1 of the trenching. In many cases a fairly complicated 'ladder' of activities and dummies is required to depict such an essentially simple situation.

The activity-on-node formulation has been generalized to give a neat solution to this problem. The meaning of Fig. 8.14 is that the concreting may not be started until 30% of the trenching is complete, and that the trenching must be completely finished before the last 10% of the concreting can be done.

Such start-to-start and finish-to-finish relationships can be shown either as a percentage of the activity concerned or in time units. A necessary delay

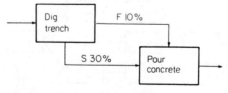

Fig. 8.14.,

between the finish of one activity and the start of another can be shown as in Fig. 8.15.

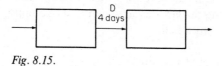

Fig. 8.15.

Many computer programmes now permit these generalized precedence relationships between activities.

Handling uncertainty

Uncertainty of activity durations

The PERT system considers activity durations as uncertain. Instead of a single estimate of each activity time, t, three estimates are asked for, defined as follows:

$$t_a = \text{shortest possible duration (most optimistic)}$$
$$t_b = \text{most likely duration (mode)}$$
$$t_c = \text{longest possible duration (most pessimistic)}$$

The usual statistical device is to assume what is known as a Beta distribution for t, which along with certain other assumptions (see Lockyer) allows the mean ($\bar{t}$) and standard deviation (s) (see Chapter 2 for definition) of the activity duration to be calculated from:

$$\bar{t} = (t_a + 4t_b + t_c)/6$$

$$s = (t_c - t_a)/6$$

Values of t for each of the activities are then used to replace the point estimates of activity durations in all the previously described calculations.

Uncertainty of project duration, t_p

By assuming that only the set of critical activities contribute to a project's uncertain duration, the project variance can be written as:

$$\text{Var}(t_p) = \sum_{i-1}^{i-N} \text{Var}(t_i)$$

where t_i is the time of the ith activity on the critical path, and N is the number of critical activities. This assumes that the durations of critical activities though uncertain are *independent* in the statistical sense, and also that no other sub-critical path can become critical (which must be strictly incorrect by the nature of the problem as now defined). Accepting the assumptions, the above formula reduces to:

Standard deviation of project duration

$$= \sqrt{\left(\sum_{i-1}^{N} S_i^2 \right)}$$

Example

Critical project duration, t(project) = 20 weeks
Standard deviation of project, s(project) = 5 weeks

What is the probability of the project duration exceeding 22 weeks? Assuming that the probability distribution of project duration is normal, and using a table of the normal distribution (see Chapter 2):

$$\frac{x}{\sigma} = \frac{t_p - t}{\sigma} = \frac{22 - 20}{5} = 0.4$$

The chance of an observation from a normal distribution being higher than the mean by more than $0.4 \times$ standard deviation is 0.165 i.e. a 1 in 6 chance.

Unfortunately the PERT assumptions can be seriously wrong. The worst trouble is caused by the assumption that there is no change in the critical path as different alternative values are taken for the activity durations. Such changes almost always cause new activities to become critical. The effect of this assumption is to give an optimistic bias to the overall project duration distribution. Typically this 'merge-event bias' leads to project duration estimates that are about 20% too low, but the error can be much greater in unfavourable cases.

Considerations such as these, together with the difficulty of obtaining and updating three times as much activity duration information, have led to a decline in the use of the three value time estimate method. The term PERT is now widely used simply as a synonym for CPM, in which single-valued activity durations are used.

Uncertainty of Network Structure

Standard network techniques assume that there is no uncertainty about the set of activities making up the network being undertaken. This assumption is manifestly untrue for certain types of project, e.g. applied research and development projects where alternative activities may be undertaken at some stage depending on the technical outcome of a previous activity. Networks that cater for chance branching are known as probabilistic networks, and the extension of arrow diagrams is sometimes known as GERT (Graphical Evaluation and Review Technique). As with standard networks, GERT networks are usually drawn with a single start and end event. Chance branching of activities as well as recycling paths can be included. In addition to the circular nodes for the logic of standard networks, chance nodes are introduced as shown in Fig. 8.16.

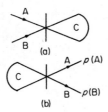

Fig. 8.16. Introduction of chance nodes. (a) Completion of either activity A or B means that the node C is reached. (b) When node C is reached, activity A or B will follow with probabilities $p(A)$ and $p(B)$ respectively, where $p(A) + p(B) = 1$.

The analysis of GERT networks is complicated. Computer programmes have been developed but they are expensive to run and are not generally available. In practice the main value of a GERT network comes from the actual process of construction which requires a thorough 'thinking through' of the project.

An example network is shown in Fig. 8.17. Note that we have included both change looping (recycling) and chance branching paths in the figure. The time taken to complete a loop can be unexpectedly long. For example, in Fig. 8.18 the average time to reach 'pass' is given by:

$$T = T_1(1-P) + 2T_1P(1-P) + 3T_1P^2(1-P) + \ldots$$

$$= T_1(1-P)\left[1 + 2P + 3P^2 + \ldots\right]$$

$$= T_1(1-P)\left[\frac{1}{(1-P)^2}\right]$$

$$= \frac{T_1}{1-P}$$

When $T_1 = 1$ week and $P = 0.8$, then $T = 5$ weeks. So it may be

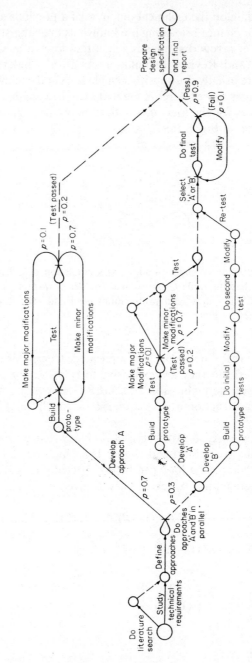

Fig. 8.17. Generalized arrow-diagram network of a project to develop a novel electronic device.

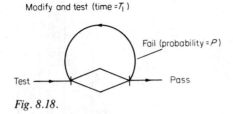

Fig. 8.18.

most important to include chance branches where these are foreseen during a project.

A different kind of generalized network has been developed by Davies. This is the Research Planning Diagram (RPD) notation which was first used for the planning and analysis of applied research projects.

Like GERT, RPD enables alternative as well as simultaneous activities to be shown, but the notation is derived from computer programming flow charts rather than from arrow diagrams. In Fig. 8.19 there is an RPD representation of the network that was shown as an arrow diagram in Fig. 8.8 and as a precedence network in Fig. 8.12.

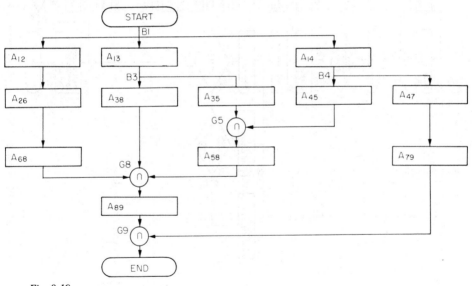

Fig. 8.19.

At first sight the RPD plan seems very similar to the precedence network. The main difference is that all events involving the convergence or divergence of parallel paths are shown explicitly in RPD. Activities have only one input arrow and only one output arrow. Parallel paths are initiated at nodes called

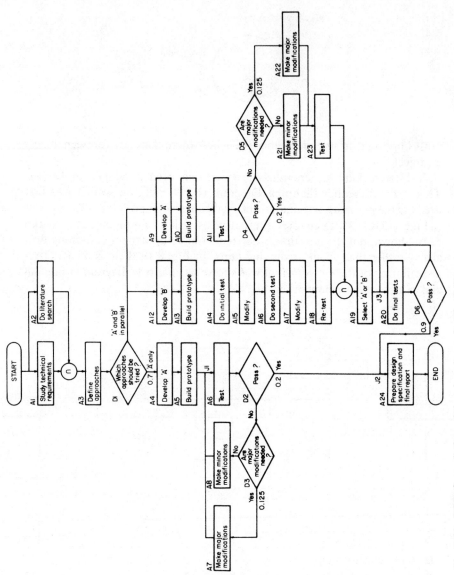

Fig. 8.20. RPD formulation of the plan shown in Fig. 8.17.

'branches' and they recombine at nodes called 'gates'. Branches B1, B3, and B4 are equivalent to the correspondingly numbered events in the arrow diagram of Fig. 8.8. Similarly the gates G5, G8, and G9 also are equivalent to arrow diagram nodes. Notice that each gate contains the logical 'AND' symbol to emphasize that all the inputs to it must be satisfied before further progress is possible.

The GERT plan of Fig. 8.17 is drawn in RPD notation in Fig. 8.20.

The major new feature compared with the deterministic plan of Fig. 8.19 is the presence of lozenge shaped 'decision' nodes. At each such node one, and only one, of the alternative output paths is taken, the choice depending on the answer to a question written inside the node. Alternative paths converage at 'junctions' such as J1, J2, and J3 in Fig. 8.20. Junctions are simply a device to reduce repetitive drawing of essentially similar features in the plan. Their major use is in the construction of loops (J1 and J3 for example).

A comparison of Fig. 8.20 with Fig. 8.17 shows that RPD gives a clearer formulation of probabilistic plans than does GERT. It is difficult to show alternatives on an arrow diagram without introducing confusing dummies and node symbols. Flow charts, on the other hand, are readily adaptable to show a variety of logical relationships, as shown by their use in many diverse technical contexts.

Probabilistic scheduling

The concepts of critical path, float, and resource scheduling are, in principle, equally applicable to probabilistic networks and to deterministic ones. Scheduling information obtained from analysis of probabilistic networks is, however, more complicated and more difficult to apply.

Referring again to Fig. 8.20, it is clear that some activities such as A3 and A24 are on the critical path. Other activities such as A12 may never be needed. The activities A12 and A18 may well be critical if they are used. However, unfavourable decisions at D4 and D5 might cause the 'A' development activities to become critical instead. If this happens the timings of A19 and A20 are thrown into doubt.

Computer programmes have been developed which can analyse RPD plans to give probabilistic information on the criticality and timing of activities, and can give probabilistic Gantt charts for the project. The application of these techniques is in its infancy, however, and more experience will be needed before simple practical rules can be devised for the effective use of this information in project management.

Project appraisal and decision analysis

Most of this chapter has been concerned with scheduling aspects of project planning, i.e. with the timing and allocation of resources to individual activities in the project.

The other major application of project planning is to the production of estimates for the project as a whole, i.e. project appraisal.

Project appraisal becomes more difficult as uncertainty grows, and the analysis of RPD plans provides a powerful means of coping with this difficulty. The analysis is based on estimates of time and cost associated with each activity, and assessments of probability at each output from a decision node. The RPD analysis programmes then calculate the probability of reading any chosen outcome to the plan as a function of the budget and of the time scale allowed for the project.

An example is shown in Fig. 8.21. Stress is laid on 'sensitivity analysis' which identifies those estimates and assessments that are crucial in determin-

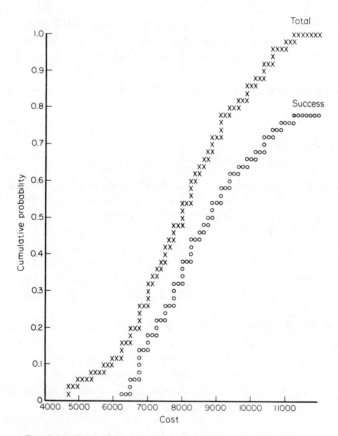

Fig. 8.21. Typical plot showing probability of completion and successful completion as a function of the budget allowed for the project.

ing the final appraisal information. These are the figures that must be examined most carefully before basing decisions on the analysis.

If numerical values can be associated with the possible outcomes of a planned project, then RPD analysis can give a complete cost-benefit picture for the project, and a choice can be made between rival projects on cost-benefit grounds.

Refinements such as time-dependent outcome values, allowance for the decision maker's attitude to risk, and discounting to present values, can be incorporated in the analysis if required.

RPD has recently been extended to include deliberate decisions. This makes it possible to model decision making situations more realistically than can be achieved using the traditional decision tree formulation.

REFERENCES

Davies, D.G.S.D., *R & D Management*, Vol. 1, No. 1, October 1970.
Lockyer, K.G., *An Introduction to Critical Path Analysis*, Pitman, 1967.

BIBLIOGRAPHY

Battersby, A., *Network Analysis for Planning and Scheduling*, Macmillan, 1964.
Crowston, W.B., "Decision CPM: network reduction and solution," *Operational Research Quarterly*, Vol. 21, No. 4, 1970.
Eisner, H., "A generalised network approach to the planning and scheduling of a research project," *Operations Research*, **10**, 1, 1962.
Elmaghraby, S.E., "An algebra for the analysis of generalised activity networks," *Management Science*, **10**, 3, 1964.
Milligan, R.A. and Brooks, D.F., "Precedence diagrams for critical path analysis," *The Engineer*, April 1968.
Pascoe, T.L., "Heuristic Methods for Allocating Resources," Ph.D. Thesis, University of Cambridge, 1965.
Thornley, G. (Ed.), *Critical Path Analysis in Practice* (collected papers on project control), Tavistock Publications, 1968.

9 Analysing Decisions

And thus the native hue of resolution
Is sicklied o'er with the pale cast of thought,
And enterprises of great pith and moment,
With this regard, their currents turn awry,
And lose the name of action.

William Shakespeare, Hamlet

In Chapter 1 it was pointed out that decision making is the prerogative of management, and O.R. workers must not expect to usurp this. However, the importance of the process is such that it is natural that O.R. workers should study it and assess how it may be improved.

Decision-making is a process in which management (in the widest sense) selects a specific course of action from a set of possible alternatives. Uncertainty is normally involved since we cannot generally be sure of the consequences of each alternative. In business, the effectiveness of a decision may be measured in money terms, but there are many situations, as we shall show, where other measures apply.

Decisions fall into a variety of types, and a non-exclusive classification is:
(1) Decisions in conditions of certainty in which all the facts and consequences are known for sure.
(2) Decisions in conditions of uncertainty where the event (or state of the system) is not known for sure (stochastic process).
(3) Decisions covering one point in time (or one time period) only.
(4) Decisions as a sequence of interrelated decisions spread out over time; this is often termed a dynamic decision problem.
(5) Decisions involving uncertainty(ies) of a natural/technical kind, where previous experience is limited or non-existent.
(6) Decisions involving uncertainty(ies) of human behaviour, such as the actions of a competitor in a common market area.

Real-world situations are enormously complex, involving technical, behavioural, economic, social, and political factors. There is literally an uncountable number of factors in most actual situations. The art, for that is what it is, of decision-taking is to *abstract* just some of the factors which are especially relevant to the decision in hand. Practical necessity forces this simplification of 'reality' if a decision is to be made that is timely. The

150

human mind cannot accept more than a few aspects of a given decision problem. The decision-taker operates with simplification as a necessary first stage.

Having selected the important features of the situation or system, and the relevant variables and relationships between them, the decision-taker combines them in some way that he would argue to be 'logical'. This combination becomes a simplified version of the real world called a 'model', and the process is one of 'model-building'. Ideally the model strips the problem of its inherent complexity while retaining the features of relevance to the decision problem. The model may be one of the following:

(1) A verbal statement of a conceptual idealization of reality which knits together the essential features.

(2) A diagrammatic (or schematic) picture such as a flow diagram or graph.

(3) A set of mathematical relationships involving the variables and specifying the situation quantitatively.

The simpler the model can be, while retaining the essential features, the better. The model will then be economical to build, understand, modify, and test. Once built, the model can be used, depending on its structure, in order to do either or both of two things:

(1) It can simulate the outcome of defined decisions, i.e. answer 'what if?' questions. This use is essentially one of simulation as a means of reaching a decision by trying things out on the model before implementing a decision in the real situation.

(2) It can seek to find the 'best' decision amongst the alternatives, implying that an operational definition of the objective exists as a part of the model's structure.

The interested reader should consult Eden and Harris (for example) for a further description and analysis of types of models and decisions.

However the model is manipulated, the decision-taker will base his decisions on it. If the logic of the model is correct, and if the relevant factors have been included, a 'good' solution will presumably be found. Even if the logic is not wholly correct, and some relevant factors are excluded, a good solution may still be reached. In practice, for reasons of practicality, this latter situation is the best that we can hope for. We have already stated that there is not time to build the perfect model. This is in any case an impossibility on philosophical grounds since the situation includes the modellers themselves in an endless interaction. An approach to the problem of model selection is given by Gillespie and Gear.

Decisions and uncertainty

We have already stated that the consequences of many significant decisions, whether in industry or the public sector, are rarely predictable with certainty. The concept of subjective probabilities based on personal or group beliefs regarding the relative weights of alternative outcomes provides a practical solution. The subjective probabilities are handled in exactly the same way from an analytical point of view as objective probabilities. (Incidentally there is some argument as to whether truly *objective* probabilities exist.)

An example

Suppose the development of a new product is under review, and that the *major* uncertainty surrounds the eventual demand. Let the fixed cost of development and tooling up be £10000 and the unit cost of production be £100. If P is the eventual profit then:

$$P = -10000 + (S - 100)X$$

where S is the selling price per unit and X is the total demand in terms of the number of units sold. Suppose the selling price is set by general market conditions as £200 per unit.

In studying the variable demand X, the decision-taker concludes that four levels may materialize, but which one actually occurs cannot be predicted with certainty until the £10000 is a 'sunk' cost. He summarizes his feelings about X with Table 9.1. For each level of sale, X, the value of P may be computed as in Table 9.2. Since the actual value of X is unknown (the true 'state of nature') it is not clear whether the £10000 fixed cost should be invested to this project or to another. A decision rule that is often used is to calculate the 'expected value' of the decision, and to go ahead if this value is higher than that of any other project that is competing for resources with the project under scrutiny.

Table 9.1.

Sales, X	Subjective probability
50	0.2
100	0.6
150	0.1
200	0.1

Table 9.2.

Sales, X	Profit, P
50	−£5,000
100	£0
150	+£5,000
200	+£10,000

Expected value

The expected value is obtained by multiplying each chance outcome (in this case profit) by the relevant subjective probability, and summing the products to form a single number, the expected monetary value. Using the example, this calculation is shown in Table 9.3.

Table 9.3.

Sales, X	Probability, p	Profit, P	$p \times P$
50	0.2	−5000	−1000
100	0.6	0	0
150	0.1	+5000	+500
200	0.1	+10000	+1000
		Total	+500

Thus, the expected monetary value of this project is + £500. Note that the value of + £500 will not actually materialize; it is purely an empirical score. However, it has the theoretical appeal that, if many decisions are taken using the expected value approach, in the absence of systematic errors in the probability assignments, the total benefit, in terms of profit of all the decisions, will tend to approach the sum of the expected values (scores) of each decision taken. Also, for the reasons discussed in Chapter 2, this sum will tend towards a normal probability distribution.

Decision rules

Some alternative decision criteria, to enable a selection of one from two or more decision options under uncertainty, are listed below:
(1) Choose the option with the highest expected value, as already outlined.
(2) Choose the option with the highest value for the most likely (i.e. highest subjective probability) outcome.
(3) Choose the option with the highest value of the lowest possible outcome (called the 'maximin' rule; this is a pessimistic attitude).
(4) Choose the option with the maximum possible outcome (called the 'maximax' rule; this is an optimistic attitude).
(5) Choose the option which maximizes the value of F in:

$$F = \text{Expected value } (E) \text{ minus a function of the degree of uncertainty}$$

e.g. max $F = E - k\sigma^2$, where k is a constant and σ^2 is the square of the standard error of the expected value based on the subjective data.

Many other rules could, of course, be chosen, and a decision-taker's attitude towards uncertainty may alter from one decision to the next. That is, the rule which describes a decision-taker's preference is essentially *situationally governed*, and the situation is constantly evolving, depending in part on previous decisions and outcomes.

At a more theoretical level, it has been suggested that a decision-taker acts so as to maximize his expected utility of the consequence(s) of a decision.

That is:

$$\text{Maximize } \exp[U(X)]$$

where $U(X)$ is the utility of X. For example, X may be money. Taking the expected value implies:

$$\text{Maximize } \sum_{i=1}^{n} p_i \, U_i \, (X_i)$$

where X takes n values, the utility of X_i is $U_i \, (X_i)$, and p_i is the probability of X_i occurring. Readers interested in this as yet theoretical concept may consult, for example, Raiffa; Schlaifer; and/or Swalm.

An illustration of this principle is the tossing of pennies for reward. Suppose that one is playing a game with an opponent. If the penny comes down heads he pays you a penny, if it comes down tails you pay him. In this game:

$$
\begin{array}{ll}
\text{Probability of success} & = \frac{1}{2} \\
\text{Value of success} & = 1\text{P} \\
\text{Probability of failure} & = \frac{1}{2} \\
\text{Cost of failure} & = 1\text{P}
\end{array}
$$

Applying the decision theory approach outlined above:

Expected Utility   =
(Probability of success × Value of success) −
(Probability of failure × Cost of failure)

Therefore:
Expected Utility $= \frac{1}{2} \times 1\text{P} - \frac{1}{2} \times 1\text{P} = 0$

One would not expect to gain or lose much from joining such a game, and one certainly would not do so with any expectation of profit. This result is in accord with experience.

Another illustration is the football pool situation. The probability of winning £75000 on the eight results with a single stake is about 1 in 73000000. The stake, which one loses anyway, is 12 P. Therefore:

$$\text{Expected Utility } = (1/73000000 \times £75000) - 12 \text{ P}$$

This is very nearly equal to -12 P and is in accordance with the common knowledge that one expects to lose one's first stake in a football pool.

Where one is comparing two situations and deciding whether to choose between them, the Expected Utility is maximized, and the actual value may not be important. For instance, if one is compelled to gamble, the tossing of pennies situation is more attractive than the football pool situation because, although the Expected Utility for tossing pennies is zero, it is nevertheless greater than that for football pools. This may explain why most people do not mind mild gambling when playing cards, although they would refuse to join a football pool syndicate. Social pressure plays a part here, of course, but even so the comparison is probably valid. Professional gamblers certainly do not make their living from football pools but gamble in situations analogous to the tossing of pennies. They usually contrive to sway the odds in their favour so that the Expected Utility is positive.

It therefore seems that this principle gives results in accordance with reality. However, there is one class of exceptions. If one had to send £5 by post one would be faced with the decision whether or not to register this amount. A decision to register would prevent a loss of £5. However:

$$\text{Expected Utility} \quad = \quad \frac{1}{50\,000} \times £5 - 45\,\text{P}$$

where $1/50\,000$ is the Post Office Corporation's figure for the proportion of lost registered letters and 45 P is the cost of registration. This Expected Utility is negative, yet in many cases one decides to register. Why?

The reason is that a certain delay ensues between posting the £5 and hearing that it has arrived safely. During this time one may be anxious about the fate of the money. Registration provides a way out of the anxiety, so in effect one ascribes a value to one's 'peace of mind' and turns the Expected Utility from negative to positive by so doing.

Note that $U(X)$ will usually be a non-linear function of X, and X may be a vector of attributes, X_1 to X_m, where m is the number of attributes. Thus $U(X)$ becomes $U(X_1, ..., X_m)$, and it may well be very difficult to deduce this function in practice. If only two or three attributes are involved the approach may become feasible.

An example of a multi-attribute problem is the selection of projects in the Ministry of Transport. Projects concerned with road safety may be evaluated in terms of the number of fatalities, serious injuries, and slight injuries prevented in the short term (say 1975–1980), the medium term (1980–1990), and the long term (beyond 1990). In this example there are 9 attributes or 'benefit areas' within which to evaluate each project. This introduces the problem of trading off objectives against each other.

Decision tree analysis

It is often necessary to take decisions regarding alternative courses of action when the outcomes of those actions are in some or all cases uncertain. Further, for a given course of action and uncertain outcome, subsequent decisions may be foreseen. Since both the uncertain outcomes and the future decisions may have an effect on the 'optimal' first-stage decision, it is essential to include this information in any analysis.

The decision tree approach is a way of displaying the anatomy of sequential decision problems. It also provides a ready means of analysing such problems. In the following section a simple example is presented before going on to a more general exposition.

Example. Plant size decisions

A single decision is considered in this problem: whether to build a small or a large plant to produce a new product. The size of the market over time can be estimated fairly accurately, but there is considerable uncertainty as to whether or not a major competitor will also produce a similar product. The data estimates for the problem are exhibited in Table 9.4 and the associated decision tree is in Fig. 9.1.

Table 9.4. 'Pay-off' table.

	Competitor does not enter field $p = 0.6$	Competitor markets a rival product $p = 0.4$
Large plant (capital cost = £80 000)	sales revenue = £150 000	sales revenue = £100 000
Small plant (capital cost = £50 000)	sales revenue = £75 000	sales revenue = £75 000

The example shows the structure of decision trees in terms of circular nodes to represent chance outcomes, square nodes to represent alternative choices open to the decision-taker, and interconnecting branches on which costs, benefits and probabilities are attached as appropriate. The tree is constructed in chronological order from left to right, while the analysis is normally carried out by working through the tree from right to left by what is known as a 'roll-back' procedure.

For the example, this amounts to calculating values at the nodes A and B, and finally C. Values can only be calculated if the decision-taker's objective function, including his attitude towards risk, are known. Assuming the decision-taker wishes to maximize expected monetary value (EMV), then the EMV's of nodes A and C are given by:

$$\text{EMV (A)} = 0.6 \times 150\,000 + 0.4 \times 100\,000 = 130\,000$$
$$\text{EMV (B)} = 0.6 \times 75\,000 + 0.4 \times 75\,000 = 75\,000$$

Node C is a conscious decision point at which the branch with the highest EMV should be selected. For the two branches from C, we have:

$$\text{EMV (large plant)} = 130\,000 - 80\,000 = 50\,000$$
$$\text{EMV (small plant)} = 75\,000 - 50\,000 = 25\,000$$

Thus, if no other considerations complicate the issue, the decision to install large plant capacity should be taken. This is indicated on Fig. 9.1 by deleting path C-B with two short bars.

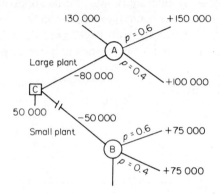

Fig. 9.1. Decision tree representation of Table 9.4.

There is, of course, no absolute answer to even the above small problem. The way in which the decision is a function of the decision rule is shown in Table 9.5

Table 9.5.

	Rule	Selection decision
1	Maximize EMV	large plant
2	Maximize value of most likely outcome	large plant
3	Maximin	small plant
4	Maximax	large plant

In the following section the ideas introduced with the small decision tree example are generalized.

Steps in Analysis

1. List decisions and uncertainties in chronological order.

2. Construct tree in consultation with decision-taker (see Fig. 9.2). This is the most difficult stage – many alternative structures may be tried until a satisfactory compromise is reached. If the tree grows large and complex, the data requirements may become greater and subject to increasing uncertainty. There seems to be art as well as science in structuring a situation at an appropriate level of detail.

3. Assign costs, benefits, and probabilities to appropriate branches. The data may be objectively, subjectively or historically based as necessary, but should represent the uncertain outcomes of decisions at each stage. Where cash flows at different points in time are involved, these should all be discounted (or accounted) to a common time, e.g. the present.

4. Analyse, perhaps using the 'roll-back' procedure, but perhaps using simulation, utility theory, or portfolio analysis (see p. 161).

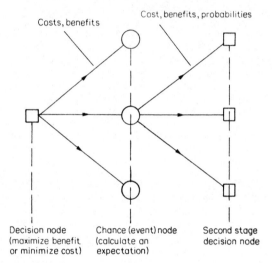

Fig. 9.2. General tree structure.

Decision tree examples

In order to demonstrate the versatility of decision tree diagramming and analysis, two examples labelled I and II are now presented, each adapted and/or disguised from actual case studies.

Case study I: Industrial project planning

In Fig. 9.3 a decision tree including several stages is shown based on a project evaluation in the chemical industry. For the purpose of presentation the number of branches emanating from chance nodes has been artificially

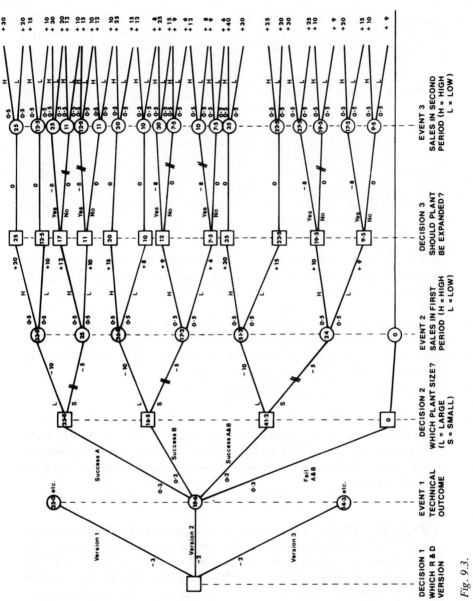

Fig. 9.3.

reduced to two only. The problem is described below:

Decision 1: this involved a choice among alternative ways (called 'versions') of carrying out the research and development aimed at marketing a new product.

Event 1: this represents the chance technical outcomes of the R & D stage. The outcomes are summarized in terms of: success for market A; success for market B; success for markets A and B; failure for markets A and B.

Decision 2: which plant size to install–large or small?

Event 2: net sales revenue in time period (first 3 years) summarized in terms of high and low sales.

Decision 3: should plant be expanded? This applies to the case of small plant installed at decision 2.

Event 3: net sales revenue in time period 2 (second 3 years).

The estimates of costs, benefits, and probabilities are shown on the branches of the tree. The results of a 'roll-back' analysis (using Max. EMV) are shown in the nodes of the tree for R & D version 2. The values are in £000's.

The analysis proceeds from right to left along the branches of the tree in exactly the same way as before. It is not a very onerous task to analyse quite large trees, using a hand calculator, in this way. In Fig. 9.3 the value in the first chance node (top right circle) is calculated from:

$$0.5(20) + 0.5(30) = 25$$

Moving to the left on the top branch, the value 25 is simply transferred since there is only the one route emanating from the square node. The value 12.5 immediately below this node is arrived at in the same way. Moving further to the left in the upper section of the tree, the value 33.8 results from the calculation:

$$0.5(25 + 20) + 0.5(12.5 + 10) = 33.8$$

The value $+20$ is the revenue from high (H) sales, and $+10$ that from low (L) sales. Moving to the left again, we reach the square node with the value 23.8 inserted. Here, since two routes are drawn, a decision is involved. The choice is between investing in a small (S) or large (L) plant at capital costs of 5 and 10 respectively. These values are shown as negative on the diagram since they are outlays. The choice is between:

$$33.8 - 10 = + 23.8 \text{ for the large plant}$$

and

$$25 - 5 = + 20 \text{ for the small plant}$$

Since we are maximizing EMV, the large plant decision is preferable;

hence the 23.8 value is entered in the square node, and the small plant route is deleted by means of the two short bars shown. Note that in this situation on the second stage decision to expand plant at a later time only occurs if the small plant option is taken at the first stage. This is reflected in Fig. 9.3.

Interestingly, in the square node with a $+9.5$ towards the bottom of the diagram, either choice (yes or no) gives the same value, i.e. $17.5-8$ and $9.5-0$ give $+9.5$. In this case the routes are equally good on Max. EMV grounds. Other factors, for example shortage of working capital, not considered in the calculation, may resolve this decision in practice. We emphasize the great ability of the decision tree method in this example to represent the project through its research and development, production, and marketing phases.

The first stage decision, relating to which technical version of the tree to follow, would appear to be a straightforward matter of choosing the greatest of:

$$\text{version 1: } 25.1-3 = 22.1$$
$$\text{version 2: } 18.6-2 = 16.6$$
$$\text{version 3: } 14.3-2 = 12.3$$

that is, version 1. In fact, version 2 was selected since there was a scarcity of skilled technical manpower. Version 2 meant that another project could also be selected and worked on simultaneously, giving the greatest overall EMV. This is an example of the importance of not considering projects in isolation. In conditions of resource scarcity(ies) it is necessary to consider the resource requirements of projects in an overall analysis, known as 'portfolio planning'. Only in this way can true global optimal decisions be approached. If there are several projects and resource scarcity(ies), some form of mathematical programming (see Chapter 7) in conjunction with decision tree diagramming may be used (Gear and Lockett).

Case study II: Educational example

Following a policy decision to 'go comprehensive', the local education authority (LEA) concerned has three major options with respect to schools A and B situated in regions S_1 and S_2 respectively of geographical area S. This situation is shown in Fig. 9.4.

The three major options are:
(1) Close B and sell the site, transferring the children at B to a comprehensive school C outside the area S by bus each day; the grammar school A would be enlarged and converted into a comprehensive to serve all the 11–16 year-olds in area S in the medium term.
(2) Convert A and B into independent comprehensives serving the 11–16 year-olds in areas S_1 and S_2 respectively.

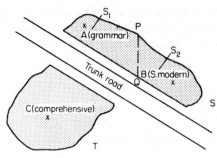

Fig. 9.4.

(3) Combine schools A and B into one comprehensive school complex for the 11–16 year-olds in area S ($= S_1 + S_2$) as a whole.

The initial policy decision and these three options are shown on the left-hand side of Fig. 9.5. Option 1 is appealing to the Council since a sum of £250000 is obtained by selling site B. It would, however, involve a high cost to enlarge A to serve area S, and necessitate bussing children now at B to C, which would overcrowd C for about 3 years. Option 1 has to gain the approval of the Department of the Environment and the Department of Education and Science as shown in the diagram. Assuming node 15 is reached, new posts would be offered for the staff at B to transfer to C. Resignations (node 26) would inevitably occur, necessitating a recruitment decision (nodes 29, 30, 31). If node 16 is reached, following refusal of permission by the D.E.S. to close school B, then the decision would be taken to follow option 3 since this would be sure to gain D.E.S. approval. The decision to combine A and B would involve the reconstitution of two organizations into one. The resignation and recruitment problems of the key headmaster would be involved, as shown from node 23 onwards.

It is worth considering Fig. 9.5 for a few minutes. Remember that the verbal descriptions of the 'nodes' (square or circular) are *boxed* while the 'activities' on the lines joining nodes are *unboxed*. Notice that the figure is constructed on a 10-year time scale from left (1972) to right (1982).

In order to check your understanding of Fig. 9.5, try to answer the following questions:

(i) Is there any doubt regarding D.E.S. approval for major option 2?

(ii) Deduce what plan 1 and plan 2, emanating from node 23, refer to?

(iii) What are the earliest and the latest times at which major option 3 can be agreed?

The answers to these questions are:

(i) Yes, there is doubt.

(ii) Plan 1 seems to be that which makes the headmaster of school B the headmaster of the new combined system, and vice versa for plan 2.

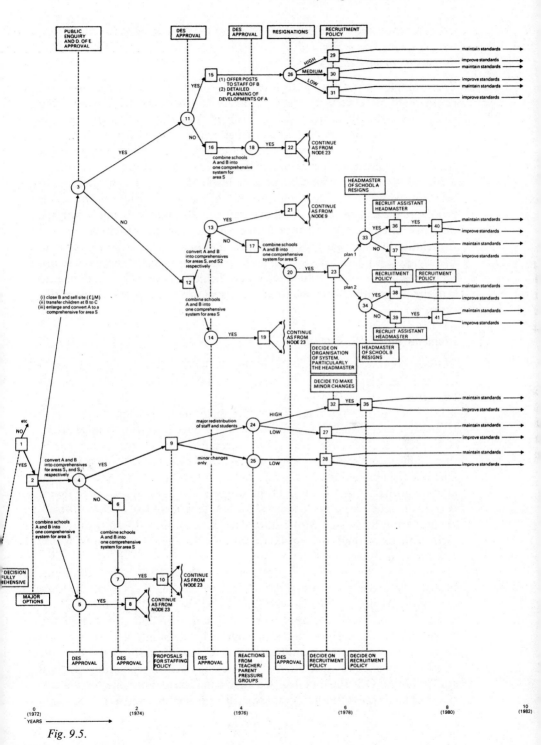

Fig. 9.5.

(iii) Earliest and latest times are 1973 and 1977 respectively.

Discussion of case studies

The examples, cases I and II, drawn from industry and the public sector respectively, pose very different problems for the analyst. The industrial study is exceedingly complex and the problem is to simplify and approximate the actual situation in order to construct a tree of manageable size. Once drawn, the analysis is relatively straightforward, as described. On the other hand, the educational problem is relatively easy to construct in the form of a tree. But acute problems, at present insoluble, arise if one attempts to attach numbers to branches and proceed with a quantitative analysis. This is because the area of educational planning is in its infancy. In particular, the objective of education, the measurement of the outputs of education, and the relationships between resource inputs and outputs are largely unknown. Clearly there is plenty of scope for management and social scientists to work on the resolution of these fundamental difficulties. However, it may be said that the unquantified tree diagram is a visual aid to decision-taking in this case.

Problems with decision trees

In this section we list some of the problems likely to be encountered during decision tree diagramming and analysis, indicating how the problems can be overcome whenever possible.

(1) The further into the future the diagram is developed, the more branches the tree has, bringing problems of data collection and analysis. An important consideration in this connection is that costs and benefits in the distant future may have small values when discounted to present time. One practical procedure is to assign values to the 'tips' of a tree terminated at some horizon date to represent the subjective opinion(s) about the future beyond the cut-off point. These values are then included in the roll-back analysis from the cut-off to the start. The essential thing to do is to experiment with more than one horizon date to see if these are sensitive to the *first* decision at 'time now' on the tree.

(2) It may be simpler to construct the tree if essentially continuous probability distributions are approximated by treating them as discrete distributions. Again, a sensitivity analysis should be carried out in which the number of discrete values approximating the distribution is increased and decreased. Alternatively a simulation approach may be adopted (see Chapter 5) in which, by repeated sampling from each distribution on the tree, the relative frequency of each alternative starting decision becoming the best can be found. One starting decision may completely dominate the rest; or the problem may be more complex, with the starting decision frequently

changing. All that can be done in the latter case is to present the results to the relevant decision-taker so that a starting decision in the face of uncertainty can be selected.

(3) The whole decision tree concept implies that *all* alternative actions are analysed, and that *all* chance outcomes are included at chance nodes. But suppose an outcome is not foreseen, and hence excluded. Then the demands of the probability concept will lead to the subjective probabilities on foreseen outcomes being arranged to sum to unity. The absence of the unforeseen path thus introduces a bias into the analysis. This is a fundamental problem to which there is no easy answer. It may sometimes be possible to incorporate a branch labelled 'unforeseen consequence', with a probability attached.

(4) It may be inappropriate to apply an individual 'roll-back' analysis to a project in isolation, since it may be important to consider several projects, sharing a common pool of scarce resources (money, manpower, facilities). This then becomes a problem of resource allocation under uncertainty applied to the project group (see Chapter 7).

(5) Care has to be taken in order to assess whether or not a particular cost or benefit should be attributed to a particular project. Questions to ask are: would the money have been spent, or the resources consumed, or the benefits accrued, independently of a given decision in the tree structure? For example, a cost may have been already committed by prior decisions to those in the analysis, in which case it becomes a future sunk cost.

(6) Different parts of an organization may be responsible for different sub-sections of the decision tree. Personnel in these areas may then each provide estimates to these sub-sections. This will lead to systematic errors between individuals due to differing attitudes towards estimation. On the other hand, the technique can have an integrating effect on the personnel concerned, improving cooperation through a common vehicle of communication – the tree diagram. In some situations it may be desirable to apply forecasting techniques to provide data (see Chapter 4), such as the Delphi technique.

The approach to decision analysis, using decision trees, does no more than suggest a systematic framework within which to analyse decisions in a consistent manner. It provides an individual faced with a problem involving choice and chance with a method that is consistent with his basic probability beliefs, preferences, and judgements.

One such method often used, albeit intuitively, by managers is the minimum principle whereby one minimises one's maximum loss. In the decision to register a letter the minimum rule says 'register'. The maximum loss is then 12p.

The minimax principle can of course be applied in situations where the outcomes of the various alternative choices cannot be expressed quantitatively, or where it is difficult to do so. Consider the perennial choice which faces all of us in a typical English summer: should I carry a mac or umbrella or not?

Here the minimax rule is applied by saying to oneself: "Which decision shall I regret more if it is the wrong one?" If you would regret carrying an umbrella or mac around, if it is a fine day, more than being caught in the rain without either if it turns out wet, then you will not take any protection. If you would regret more being caught in the rain, then you take an umbrella.

Clearly the choice depends on circumstances. If you ride around in a car and at worst would only have a short dash in a shower of rain, the preference may be not to take the mac. If you would be seriously inconvenienced in rain, then you protect yourself.

The choice also depends upon probabilities. If the sky in the morning appears overcast, the decision will be weighted in favour of the mac. If the sky has been cloudless for days, only a pessimist would bother. Thus these decision functions can be applied even in qualitative situations.

It is important for a managing director to appreciate that the minimax rule is probably being intuitively applied by many of his staff in making their day-to-day decisions. In the lower strata of the executive structure, safety first is a much more powerful watchword than the maximization of Expected Utility which may, as shown above, be far more advantageous to the company where repetitive judgements are required. Stock control is the prime example of the minimax attitude. It may benefit the company financially to allow 5% of its products to be out of stock, but an individual stock controller often dare not make this decision. It should, very properly, be made by the managing director, who, aware of the damaging effect that the minimax rule may have in such situations, should see to it that the appropriate rule for maximization of Expected Utility is teased out and applied.

To sum up, it might be said that, if you are faced occasionally with decisions whose outcome could result in substantial losses, then the minimax rule is a good one to apply, but if you have a succession of such decisions to take, then a maximization of the expected utility is appropriate.

REFERENCES

Eden, C. and Harris, J., *Management Decision and Decision Analysis*, Macmillan, 1975.
Gillespie, J.S. and Gear, A.E., *IEEE Trans. on Eng. Management*, Vol. EM-20, No. 4, 1973.
Raiffa, H., *Decision Analysis: Introductory Lectures on Choices Under Uncertainty*, Addison-Wesley, 1968.
Magee, J.F., *Harvard Business Review*, July/Aug. 1964, pp. 144–156.
Moore, P.T. *et al.*, *Case Studies in Decision Analysis*, Penguin Books, 1976.
Schlaifer, R., *Probability and Statistics for Business Decisions*, (Chapter 4), McGraw-Hill, 1959.
Swalm, R.O., *Harvard Business Review*, **44**, No. 6, 1966.
Gear, A.E. and Lockett, A.G., *IEEE Trans on Eng. Management*, Vol. EM-20, No. 1, 1973.

10 Operational Gaming

No game was ever yet worth a rap,
For a rational man to play,
Into which no accident, no mishap,
Could possibly find its way.

A.L. Gordon, Ye Weary Wayfarer

In Chapter 5 we looked at the use of simulation techniques (Monte Carlo, deterministic and industrial dynamics) for conducting experiment on models that describe elements of business, organizational, and economic models. In all these cases the main effort is necessary in the initial descriptive stage, i.e. building a model. Once it is built and checked it can then be run and different environments tested by changing various parameters. In all cases the results are usually given without managerial intervention. There are situations, however, where it is not completely possible to simulate the complete decision process, or where we may want to study how managers make decisions. Some very interesting work of this kind has been done on the information flow in a steel-making plant. Amiry, Mellor, and Hopkins have written about various aspects of the simulation which they termed a production game.

The problem they looked at was that of the information necessary to 'best' control a steelworks. In the dynamic industrial system decisions have to be made now which take into account some forecasts of the future. Any such information is bound to be subject to error. This may be due to inherent uncertainty of the process or due to the time lag of the information. More up-to-date information can be provided to the controller, i.e. the time lag reduced, but the cost will rise. The problem is to strike an economic balance between the costs of communications and the use which a controller can make of the information.

To study the information system in action a partial model of the controller's office was made including actual display boards. These showed the present state of the plant and forecast times when furnaces would require charging and action had to be taken. The actual figures were provided from a simulation model of the plant run on a computer. But when decisions about the plant operation, such as which crane to use, were required, management made the decision. This information was then fed back into the computer. The plant controller became part of the total simulation, and his actions and use of information could be studied under controlled conditions. In this particular plant, the output had risen substantially (by nearly 75%) with very little change in manning and "a study of the present information flow showed certain weaknesses in the communication system".

The basic problem was that of crane utilization and conflicting operations. Cranes were used to put molten iron into the mixer (a large vessel holding a stock of molten iron – unlike the portable 'torpedoes' we mentioned during our discussion of a Monte Carlo simulation) and pour it into furnaces. Because the cranes can 'interfere' with each other there often arose a conflict of interests.

Let us look at a very 'stylized' example to show what can occur. Consider a plant having 4 furnaces and 2 cranes as shown in Figs. 10.1–10.3. If furnace 4 wants molten iron this may be supplied by crane 2. First it has to take some metal from the mixer. Crane 1 moves to the left-hand side out of the way (see Fig. 10.1). In Fig. 10.2 we see that furnace 1 has tapped and now requires charging. Crane 1 is getting metal from the mixer while Crane 2 is putting its molten iron into furnace 4, i.e. charging furnace 4. The next figure shows how the cranes interfere. Crane 2 has finished charging

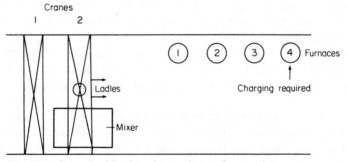

Fig. 10.1. Crane 2 taking iron from mixer to furnace 4.

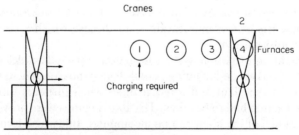

Fig. 10.2. Furnace 1 requests metal.

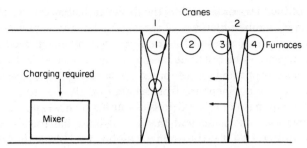

Fig. 10.3. Mixer requires charging, but crane 2 cannot get past crane 1.

and has nothing to do. If crane 1 was not charging the first furnace it could be charging iron from the blast furnaces into the mixer. Therefore there is the likelihood of a delay in metal supply from the mixer at some later date. This could have been avoided if furnace 1 was charged by the second crane as well – but this would have meant some delay in charging the furnace because it was still working on furnace 4. It is a question of balancing present loss against future expected gain. The decision to charge a furnace now has to take into account when other actions are expected to be necessary. Changing the information, i.e. keeping it more up-to-date, may affect the 'quality' of the decision.

Using the man-machine simulation we have described, we see how alterations to the speed of information flow could be made and their effect quickly tested. Increasing the speed costs money and there comes a point where the extra benefit is not worth the increase in cost. What is required is the cheapest system overall, which we have referred to from time to time in earlier chapters. This is where O.R. is very powerful, taking a broad overall look at the system under consideration.

A detailed description of the particular problem we have looked at is given in Amiry for the interested reader.

Military gaming

The production game we have just looked at involved conflict between various actions. It could be called a 'game against Nature', because the conflict was not between players, i.e. human decision-makers, but was due to the involved nature of the system under consideration. In some cases the conflict is directly between interested parties. Such instances occur when we look at military games and business management games. They are the most widely used forms of what is known as 'operational gaming', where players or decision-makers act within the simulated environment, and the experimenter, by observing them, may be able to test hypotheses concerning the behaviour of the individuals and/or the decision system as a whole. We will look at military gaming first.

This is essentially a method for training whereby alternative attack and defence strategies can be tested against opponents. The typical simple game has two teams or opposing sets of forces, and a very good description can be found in the article by Shephard from which Figs. 10.4 to 10.6 are adapted. Each side usually has complete details about his own weapons, but incomplete information otherwise, and this necessitates the use of intelligence operations. In Fig. 10.4 it is shown in a simplified way how the information between the two teams flows, and it illustrates how the various factors are interdependent. An early form of the game has just one battlefield as illustrated in Fig. 10.5. Each commander (usually called Blue and Red for convenience) gets information about his own troops and weapons, and receives 'intelligence' about the enemy which is usually incomplete, if not misleading. Given this state of affairs he has then to command his forces. A set of rules has to be drawn up so that no one can 'cheat', and this necessitates having an umpire, called 'control'. The commanders are given separate rooms and a model of the terrain, giving positions of the two opposing forces as shown in Fig. 10.6. They do not directly interact with one another but pass their decisions into the control section. The game may continue for as long as is wished, and the rules may become very complex. In the situations described by Shephard the rule book had over 100 pages, and was 'based on the results

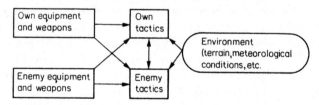

Fig. 10.4., Information flows between teams.

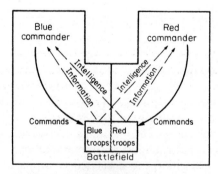

Fig. 10.5. Example game structure.

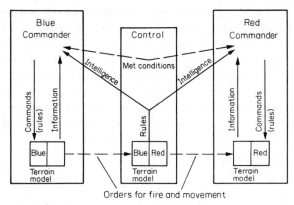

Fig. 10.6. Game operating system.

of analyses of past operations, on scientific assessment, and on data obtained from field trials and exercises'. Use of such gaming techniques enables junior officers to get a feel for situations that they have not experienced or are unlikely to experience unless involved in battle. Very realistic situations can be created by the use of such devices as proper documentation, and re-living 'old battles'. For today's warfare, combined operations of air, sea, and land forces are often required. Such situations often necessitate the use of a computer to handle the vast amount of information and can be very costly exercises–but the concepts are essentially as we have just described.

Business games

The most commonly known form of gaming is the business game, which is a type of educational tool for training managers (or managers to be). Many forms of business game can now be found, and Management Departments or Business Schools in Universities, computer manufacturers, and many large companies have developed their own to suit their particular needs. A National Management game is played annually in the *Financial Times*. In the early stages of development, Operational Researchers were deeply involved, but today this is not always the case. The games usually involve a number of teams who act as managers of companies competing against each other. Each team has to make decisions from time to time on factors such as price, marketing and R & D expenditure, distribution channels, etc. These decisions are fed into a model of the economic environment and the results are then fed back to each team for further action.

A very good example which we will describe is Simulex, developed by Wood, which will illustrate the typical level of complexity that is involved. In the model a number of firms make and market a semi-durable consumer product. These different brands compete for the market; there are also other brands marketed by other firms in the game but they are a background market and are allowed for in the model on which the calculations are based. This allows the game to be partially competitive, but also allows careful analysis of the implications of each decision to be rewarded. The model used is constructed such that current profits have to be balanced against future profits. There are certain resource constraints which need to be anticipated in advance if future growth (i.e. expansion) is to prove economical.

Table 10.1 A typical balance sheet.

	£	£	£
CAPITAL EMPLOYED			
Issued Equities			10 000 000
Capital Reserve & Share Premium A/C			3 500 000
Unappropriated Profit			2 527 173
Debenture Stock			5 000 000
USE OF CAPITAL			
Fixed Assets			
Buildings		2 000 000	
Machinery, value at year start	11 196 000		
Additions during year	2 464 000		
Less depreciation	1 060 000		
Machinery, value at year end		12 600 000	
Current Assets			
Opening value, stocks of comps & W.I.P.	451 000		
Stock Changes During Year	405 440		
Closing value, stocks of comps & W.I.P.		856 440	
Cash and bank balances		5 570 733	
Current Liabilities			
Taxation provision			0
Dividend declared			0
Debenture interest provision			0
		21 027 173	21 027 173

Signed on behalf of the Board

—————————————————Director

—————————————————Director

At the beginning of the game each team is given an opening balance sheet which shows the general position of the company (Table 10.1), an industrial bulletin giving some historical information (Table 10.2), and a detailed profit and loss statement for the last period (Table 10.3). After studying the initial information and making sure they understand the game, each team then has to fill in a decision form like that shown in Table 10.4.

Table 10.2. Industrial Bulletin

	Year 1	Year 2	Year 3	Year 4	Year 5 in quarters	
					1	2
Predicted value of G.N.P.*	102.0	100.0	100.0	103.5	104.3	106.8
Actual value of G.N.P.	97.3	98.3	100	103.2	104.4	105.15
Price movements and range	£100–150	90–110	80–90	75–85		75–85
Gross expenditure on marketing	£m 1.5	1.7	3.2	7.1		18.2
Sales revenue for the industry	£m 15	44	88	185		395

			Year 6 in quarters			
	3	4	1	2	3	4
Predicted value of G.N.P.*	106.0	108.85	107.7	108.55	109.4	109.9
Actual value of G.N.P.	105.95	106.8				

* This figure represents the most recent predicted value of G.N.P. available.

Price of machine tools first period Year 6 will be £22 750 and £23 000, £23 000, £23 250 in the second, third and fourth periods respectively. We expect that the industry will achieve a 65% penetration of the market by the beginning of Year 9. It seems unlikely that it will be possible to achieve a higher target than this in the following years.

Price of bought-in components will be £63 in period one, year 6.

Every period (a quarter of a year) each team has to decide:

(1) The amount to make in each area (provided that there is a factory in that area).

(2) Rate of machine tool usage.

(3) The quantities of products to be transported between the various areas.

(4) New machine tools to be ordered.

(5) The amount to be spent on marketing.

(6) Selling price.

(7) The number of dealers to be used, i.e. the number of distribution channels.

(8) Financial information concerning stocks and shares, and also the amount of profit given out to shareholders.

Table 10.3. Initial company position. All firms

PROFIT AND LOSS STATEMENT		CASH FLOW STATEMENT	
Transport costs	320000	Cash available	1453265
Direct prod costs	2362000	Less cash expenses	4112769
Cost of components	178500	Min cash avail	−2659504
Cost of M.T. hire	0	Add sales revenue	4432714
Dir lab and mktg costs	1150000	Less new investment	675000
		Less dividend	0
Total	4010500	Less deb interest	0
		Less tax paid	27477
Short term interest	102269	Add val new deb	4500000
Debenture interest	0	Add val new eq iss	0
Depreciation	315000	Net cash flow	4117468
Total	4427769	New cash avail next period	5570733
Less change stk val	218750		
Total cost goods sold	4209009		
Sales Revenue	4432714		
Trading profit	223705		
Invest al and loss c/f	168750		
Tax	27477	Investment allowance and	
Net income	196228	Tax loss carried forward	0

Table 10.4. Simulex decision form

Period ⑦② Team Ⓔ

Order for bought in components ☐⑥⑤⓪⓪ batches

	Area 1	Area 2	Area 3	Area 4
Quantity to be manufactured in area (000's)	①③⓪	☐☐⓪	☐☐⓪	☐☐⓪
Number of machine tools to be used	⑨①②	☐☐⓪	☐☐⓪	☐☐⓪
Number of units to be shipped in (+) or out (−) (000's). (This row must total to zero)	⊟☐⑨⑦⑤	⊞☐②⑤⓪	⊞☐④⑤⓪	⊞☐②⑦⑤
Number of machine tools ordered	☐☐☐⓪	☐☐☐⓪	☐☐☐⓪	☐☐☐⓪
Marketing expenditure (£'000)	☐②④⓪	☐②④⑤	☐③②⓪	☐②④⑤
Unit selling price, £	⑦⑨	⑧②	⑧⓪	⑧⓪
Number of dealers	☐☐③	☐☐⓪	☐☐⑧	☐☐☐

	Nominal	Cash value
Capital issues debentures	①⑤⓪⓪⓪⓪⓪⓪	①③⑤⓪⓪⓪⓪⓪
Equity	☐☐☐☐☐☐☐⓪	☐☐☐☐☐☐☐⓪

Dividend declared ☐⓪☐ %

About an hour is allowed for each decision period, and the teams, usually consisting of 6 or 7 people, have to work hard in keeping track of events. After the decision has been made, the forms are collected by the controller and fed into the model. This produces statements showing the present position of each team; a typical example is given in Table 10.5. We have not the space to discuss the game in great detail here, but hope you have some of the flavour. Events can get very complex and detailed, such as rival teams 'buying out' some of the opposition. The whole game becomes very realistic and participants can get very involved. Although the computer is used to help in the analysis, the controller himself has to simulate roles such as banker, which cannot easily be computerised.

Table 10.5. Detailed position of company given at beginning of each period

Team Number 1

Period 2	Production					Sales			
	Area 1	Area 2	Area 3	Area 4		Area 1	Area 2	Area 3	Area 4
Prodn	72	0	0	0	Dealers	12	9	9	2
% change	10.7	0.0	0.0	0.0	Mkt 000	160	135	145	60
Mt used	602	0	0	0	Price	78.00	82.00	85.00	78.00
Shipments	50.0	20.0	20.0	10.0	Av mkt	135	120	115	100
Mt order	100	0	0	0	Av price	82.60	82.00	81.50	81.00
New mt av	687	0	0	0	Pr sales	19421	18247	15813	0
D. cost unit	38.69	0.00	0.00	0.00	Init stk	10716	9890	12324	0
Tot dir cst	2786	0 ..	0	0	Clos stk	2716	9384	18679	5676
Trnsprt est	0	160	160	80	Sales	30000	20506	13645	4324

Components		Machine tools			
Order	4000	Machine tool price	23000		
List price	57.0	Depreciation No.	15	Cost	345000
Contract price	55.0	Investment No.	100	Cost	2300000
Close st	1150	Tool hire No.	0	Cost	0
Tot cost	220000				

Profit and loss statement		2 Quarter	Cash flow statement
Transport costs	400000	Cash available	4726229
Dir prod costs	2786120	Less cash expenses	4871716
Cost of components	220000	Min cash avail	−145487
Cost of m.t. hire	0	Add sales revenue	5518589
Dir and mktg costs	1460000	Less new investment	2300000
Total	4866120	Less dividend	0
Short term interest	5595	Less deb interest	0
Debenture interest	100000	Less tax paid	0
Depreciation	345000	Add val new deb	0
Total	5316716	Add val new eq iss	0
Less stock change	163000	Net cash flow	−1653127
Tot cost of sales	5153716	New cash available	3073102
Sales revenue	5518589	Tax loss c/f	288618
Trading profit	364873		
Tax loss b/f	653491		
Tax	0		
Net income	364873		

As well as using the exercise to help train managers, it has been used to study how managers decide. Eccles analysed the decisions made by many different participants who have played the game. He has controlled the game as though it were a scientific experiment in a laboratory, and hence used it as a research tool.

War games are now one of the biggest military applications of operational research; they are regularly played at NATO, the US Strategic Command, and no doubt in Russia and China too. Perhaps, after all, Arthur Clarke was right when he defined O.R. as the art of winning wars without actually fighting.

Playing business games between different sections of the same company provides valuable lessons as to the guiding philosophy behind the policies of each of these sections. One finds that the sales organization team tends to keep prices low. A research organization team tends to experiment, perhaps not always wisely. A production control team tends to concentrate on inventory stability and overlook opportunities for increasing sales. With these narrow conceptions exposed in the genuinely competitive atmosphere of a business game, each section of the company learns the necessity to take an overall view and appreciate more fully the need for sales forecasts in regulating production, the value of research in promoting sales, the necessity for reconciling apparently conflicting objectives, and so on. As one work study manager said after finishing a game, 'I feel much more sympathy for my managing director now'.

These models can be used with great effect to test out O.R. policies and even to train O.R. workers! They have the virtue of organizational flexibility also in that intensive sessions of play can be carried out over one or two days of complete separation from normal duties, or longer periods of play can be arranged without distraction from normal work, the players making their decisions in the time that they would usually spend on crossword puzzles, and then sending the results to a central agency to be computed and returned for further decisions in due course.

A very interesting new model has been developed by Willmer which is called Machiavellian Dynamics. It is a very simple device which may be used to demonstrate the conflicting ideas of power and cooperation in a competitive environment.

Each group is assigned a 'board-room' where they can discuss policy and strategy without interference from other teams. A separate room is used for discussions between the groups and also for the submission of contract sheets to the adjudicator. A sample contract sheet is shown in Fig. 10.7; this must be correctly completed and signed by the group representative before it is submitted. Each group must name their own representative before the start of the first period.

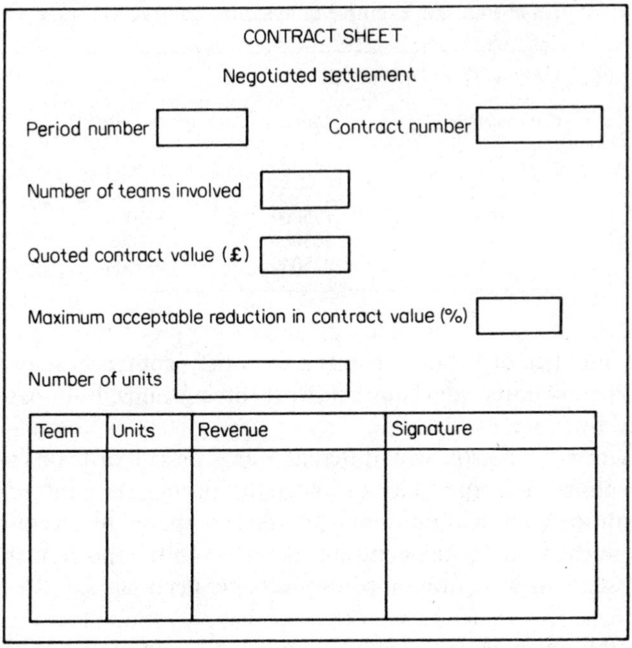

CONTRACT SHEET

Negotiated settlement

Period number [   ]   Contract number [   ]

Number of teams involved [   ]

Quoted contract value (£) [   ]

Maximum acceptable reduction in contract value (%) [   ]

Number of units [   ]

Team	Units	Revenue	Signature

Fig. 10.7. Sample contract sheet.

At the beginning of each period, all groups are subject to the following conditions:

(1) A fixed cost of £10 000 is automatically incurred, whether units are used or not.

(2) There is a production capacity of 100000 units per period, and unused capacity cannot be carried forward.

(3) Variable production cost is £1 per unit.

(4) If a team has to supply more than 100 000 units in any one period, the extra units are automatically bought in at a cost of £3 each. In general, therefore, over-production is to be avoided, but in some cases it will still be possible to make a profit on the extra units, depending on the agreed revenue split.

A list of available contracts, similar to that shown in Table 10.6 is circulated at the start of each period, and the following are points to note:

(1) The total number of units required in any one contract list may be less than or exceed the total capacity of the groups.

(2) The profitability of the various contracts, even within the same list, may be quite different.

Table 10.6. An example of available contracts

Contract list – Period 4		
Contract No.	*Units*	*Revenue (£)*
1	95000	140000
2	110000	180000
3	195000	300000
4	205000	305000
5	225000	400000

(3) The number of groups required to satisfy contracts may vary. For example, 205000 units will require at least three groups, but obviously may be satisfied by more.

(4) There is no reason why different teams or sets of teams should not submit sheets for the same contract. When this occurs, the contract is awarded to a coalition chosen at random from those prepared to accept the cogent reduction in the value of the contract. It is therefore important that groups have up-to-date information on contracts being negotiated.

The overall objective is the maximization of accumulated profit. In each period several fixed price contracts are offered which require a certain number of 'units' and guarantee a particular revenue. The groups must bargain amongst themselves and form coalitions to satisfy the contracts, stating how the units and revenue will be split. Some contracts will be small enough to enable one group to satisfy them, but the majority will require the cooperation of two or more teams. Any profit generated is carried forward to the following period.

Although an overall objective has been imposed, this is in no way meant to be rigid. Teams are at liberty to follow strategies consistent with a completely different objective. For example, group 'A' may choose to ensure that group 'B' has a low profit level, whatever the consequences.

To encourage the groups to take advantage of positions of bargaining power, a tax has been introduced which penalizes the 'fair-play, equal-shares' approach. This tax comes into operation when two or more teams undertake a contract and the revenue is split in approximately the same ratio as the units. For example, a contract of 100000 units worth £150000 supplied by two teams each contributing 50000 units and receiving £75000 would be subject to fair-play' tax.

The tax amounts to about 10% of the revenue involved, and so for a large contract will represent an appreciable loss in profit. It is unlikely that in any situation the bargaining groups will have exactly equal power, and it is expected that this potential penalty will encourage teams to perform the

Table 10.7.

PERIOD NUMBER 5		
CONTRACTS NOT ACCEPTED:		
Contract Number		Teams involved
1		2
4		1
PENALTIES INCURRED THIS PERIOD:		
Team Number		Penalty
1		2000
2		0
3		3000
4		0
PERIOD AND CUMULATIVE PROFIT FIGURES:		
Team Number	Profit this period	Profit to date
1	12000	16600
2	10000	205000
3	87000	320000
4	30000	140000

usually simple analysis required to establish the relative power positions.

After the decision sheets have been completed and analysed, the groups are given the present state of the situation, as exampled by Table 10.7.

This game is different from the earlier one that we described because it concentrates mainly on power and bargaining, and very little on numerate, financial, and other skills. In essence it is a simulation of an *N*-person game. It is a fascinating experience to see the effect it has on the players, and the results are far from predictable.

REFERENCES & BIBLIOGRAPHY

Amiry, A.P., "The simulation of information flow in a steelmaking plant, in Digital simulation in operational research," pp. 157–165.

Eccles, A.J. and Wood, D., "How Do Managers Decide," *J. Manag. Studies*, Vol. 9, No. 3, 1972, pp. 291–302.

Hopkins, D.A., "Controlled display facilities for simulation games," in *Digital Simulation in Operational Research*, E.U.P., 1967, pp. 347–354.

Mellor, P. and Tocher, K.P., "A steel works production game," *O.R.Q.*, Vol. 14, No. 2, 1963.

Willmer, M.A.P. and Westwood, J.B., *Machiavellian Dynamics*, Manchester Business School, Manchester.

Wood, D., *Simulex: A Management Simulation Exercise*, Manchester Business School, Manchester.

Hollingdale, S.H. (Ed.), *Digital Simulation in Operational Research*, E.U.P., 1967 and Shephard, R.A., pp. 210–217.

Naylor, T.H., Bibliography 19, "Simulation and Gaming," *Computing Reviews*, January 1969, pp. 61–69.

11 Other Techniques of Relevance to O.R.

For nothing goes for sense, or light,
That will not with old rules jump right,
As if rules were not in the schools
Derived from truth, but truth from rules.

Samuel Butler, Hudibras

In this chapter we attempt to summarize O.R. related techniques not so far included, providing further references where appropriate. More complete lists of definitions of management techniques can be found in the following books:

A New Glossary of Management Techniques, by John Argenti and Crispin Robe, published by Management Publications Ltd., 1967.

The Encyclopedia of Management, by Carl Heyel, published by Van Nostrand Reinhold Co., 1973.

A Handbook of Management, by Thomas Kempner, published by Weidenfeld and Nicolson, 1971.

The Techniques of Business Control, by F. Clive de Paula and A.W. Willsmore, published by Pitman, 1973.

Corporate planning

Corporate planning is concerned with the determination of a set of goals and objectives for an organization treated as a whole, and with the generation and examination of alternative ways of achieving goals and objectives, taking account of internally and externally set constraints. The main advantages of introducing this approach are claimed to be:

(i) A clearer understanding of the trade-offs involved between alternative sets of activities, especially in conditions of scarce resources such as manpower, money, and facilities.

(ii) Improved communication between traditionally separated functional areas such as finance, production, marketing, personnel, and research and development.

REFERENCES

Ansoff, H.I., *Corporate Strategy*, McGraw-Hill, 1965.
Argenti, J., *Systematic Corporate Planning*, Nelson, 1974.

Discounted cash flow (DCF) methods

It is important when assessing investment projects that the criteria used adequately reflect the time value of money whether outgoings or incomings. Firms using the pay-back method estimate the time that will be required for a project's profits to just recoup the investment. The shorter this time the better the project. The main weaknesses of this approach are that no account is taken of the timing of returns during the pay-back period, and that returns after this time are not considered.

The advantages of DCF methods for determining the value of a project are:

(a) Account is taken of the complete stream of cash flows over the life of the project.

(b) Account is taken of the fact that £100 is worth more today than £100 in, say, a year's time.

The main DCF methods involve the calculation of a net present value (NPV) or of a rate of return (ROR). Both methods stem from a common theoretical base.

The net present value method assumes that the appropriate cost of capital to finance investment at the margin is known, and projects are accepted that have the largest positive NPVs. The rate of return calculation involves finding the highest rate of interest that the project cash flows can bear before starting to show a deficit in terms of NPV. Provided that the cost of capital is less than the rate of return, the project is deemed worth doing in general.

Formulas

(i)   The net present value of an investment proposal is defined symbolically as:

$$\text{NPV} = C_0 + \frac{C_1}{(1 + r_0)} + \frac{C_2}{(1 + r_0)^2} + \dots + \frac{C_n}{(1 + r_0)^n}$$

where $C_0, C_1, \dots, C_n$ are *net* cash *inflows* for years $n = 0, 1, 2, \dots, n$, and n is the number of years of the project's life. The discount rate, r_0, is the cost of capital reflecting the appropriate cost of finance for the project.

(ii)   The DCF rate of return, r, is defined as the discount rate that results in making the net present value of all the cash flows for the project equal zero. That is, r is found by solving the equation:

$$\text{NPV} = 0 = C_0 + \frac{C_1}{(1+r)} + \frac{C_2}{(1+r)^2} + \ldots + \frac{C_n}{(1+r)^n}$$

Example

It is proposed to buy an item of machinery for an outlay of £1 200 immediately. The machine will change a production process by making more efficient use of a raw material. Net cash savings if the machine is acquired are estimated as shown in Table 11.1 for each of years 1 to 8 inclusive.

The computations for discount rates of 6%, 10%, and 15% are also shown in Table 11.1. The NPVs at these rates are represented in Fig. 11.1.

Table 11.1. Example of cash flows for a project

Year	0	1	2	3	4	5	6	7	8	Discounted totals
Cash flow	−1200	+200	+300	+300	+250	+200	+100	+50	+300	
Discount factor at 6%	1.000	0.943	0.890	0.840	0.792	0.747	0.705	0.665	0.627	
Cash flow at 6%	−1200	+188.6	+267	+252	+198	+149.4	+70.5	+33.3	+188.1	+146
Discount factor at 10%	1.000	0.926	0.857	0.794	0.735	0.681	0.630	0.583	0.540	
Cash flow at 10%	−1200	+185.2	+257.1	+238.2	+183.8	+136.2	+63	+29.2	+162	+55
Discount factor at 15%	1.000	0.870	0.756	0.658	0.572	0.497	0.432	0.376	0.327	
Cash flow at 15%	−1200	+174	+226.8	+197.4	+144	+99.4	+43.2	+18.8	+98.1	−198

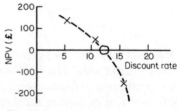

Fig. 11.1.

Thus, for example, the NPV at 6% is $+146$. If the cost of capital is less than or equal to 6% the project is certainly worth doing. The NPV $= 0$ at a discount rate of around 12%, which is the rate of return of the project. The project is worth doing if interest charges are less than 12%.

Assumptions and problems

(a) The discount rate (cost of capital) is usually assumed to be the same for cash flows connected with a project's cost as for a project's benefits.

(b) The discount rate is usually assumed to be constant, independent of time.

(c) Calculation of an ROR through the equation NPV $= 0$ can lead to an equation for r with more than one solution. However, this is not a common problem and arises only if further substantial outlays are involved after some benefits have started to come in.

(d) Projects with benefits in the more distant future are viewed less favourably after discounting than those with shorter term returns.

(e) As described in these notes, problems of uncertainty connected with the cash flows are not included.

(f) Under conditions of shortage of resources, e.g. scarcity of investment capital, the criteria of NPV and ROR applied to individual projects leads to sub-optimal decisions in general.

REFERENCES

Kingshott, A.L., *Investment Appraisal*, Ford Motor Co., 1967.
Merrett and Sykes, *The Finance and Analysis of Capital Projects*, Longmans, 1963.

Cost-benefit analysis

This is an evaluation technique usually applied to large projects. An attempt is made to quantify all the costs and benefits in terms of money. For example, in deciding on the routing of a new motorway the value of time saved by users, and the value of lives saved and/or lost would be taken into account, as well as the direct cost of the road building programme itself. Problems of definition arise such as whether to list a dis-benefit as a cost. More fundamentally, economists are undecided as to the methodology of arriving at unit prices of time saved, lives lost, etc.

The closely related technique of cost-effectiveness analysis is sometimes employed when the value or benefits of a project cannot be measured in terms of money. The stage when this situation exists is open to argument, involving a whole academic area, Welfare Economics.

REFERENCES

Goldman, T.A., *Cost Effectiveness Analysis*, Praeger, 1967.
Peters, G.H., *Cost Benefit Analysis and Public Expenditure*, Institute of Economic Affairs, 1966.

Output budgeting

There is some confusion in the literature regarding differences between a number of closely related techniques. We shall use the term Output Budgeting as synonymous with Programme Budgeting, and Planning Programming Budgeting System. These are not techniques for decision-taking themselves, but seek to provide a framework within which decisions can be identified and analysed. The principal stages in Output Budgeting are:

(1) Develop strategic objectives of an organization as a whole.

(2) Interpret strategic objectives in terms of shorter term sub-objectives and goals.

(3) Identify outputs of the organization and define measures of output achievement.

(4) Identify activities that contribute towards goals.

(5) Define the availability of resources of every kind.

(6) Develop groups of activities that form viable programmes (i.e. viable in the light of resources required and constraints of a statutory, social, political, etc. nature).

(7) Analyse alternative programmes in order to reach a decision regarding which one to adopt for the coming time period (e.g. coming year).

(8) Develop a detailed activity plan/schedule for the adopted programme which includes a budget plan.

(9) Implement the plan and monitor achievement of goals.

(10) Review progress and re-cycle through the above stages whenever necessary as actual outputs differ from planned outputs/achievements.

REFERENCES

Merewitz, L. and Sosnick, S.H., *The Budget's New Clothes*, Markham, 1971.
Novick, D., *Program Budgeting*, Harvard University Press, 1965.
Output Budgeting for the Department of Education and Science, Department of Education and Science, HMSO, London, 1970.

Management by objectives (MBO)

This technique, as its title implies, focuses on the objectives and sub-objectives of an organization. It has been said that MBO is more an attitude of mind than a technique, but nevertheless some stages can be identified as follows:

1. Agree policy, i.e. aims (long-term) of the organization.
2. Check that the organization is capable of working towards the stated aims.
3. Establish functional (operational) objectives for each area of the organization in keeping with the long-term aims, emphasizing results in a quantitative form if possible.
4. Discuss the functional (operational) objectives of (3) with key subordinates with a view to establishing their sub-objectives.
5. Ensure that the process of agreeing objectives at lower management levels is implemented.
6. Decide upon activities to attain stated objectives and goals.
7. Define procedures for feeding back information at all levels in the organization to ensure a review of progress towards the achievement of objectives, goals, and targets.
8. Re-cycle through steps (1) to (7) inclusive as the need to adapt plans to a changing situation becomes apparent from the information feedback system.

The emphasis is, then, upon the definition and refinement of working objectives and activities for everyone in the organization, in the light of its overall aims. However, it should be noted that Output Budgeting and Management by Objectives have many common elements. Both are intended to aid the management of complex organizations under conditions of uncertainty and in a climate in which multiple objectives exist. There is a significant difference of emphasis between the techniques in that Management by Objectives focuses attention on structuring the setting of operational objectives by means of exchanges between managers and subordinates at various levels of management; i.e. it emphasizes the agreements as a continuing dynamic process.

REFERENCES

Humble, J.W., *Improving Business Results*, McGraw-Hill, 1968.
Reddin, W.J., *Effective MBO*, Management Publications Ltd., London, 1971.

Cybernetics

Most industrial operations need regulation, and substantial strides have been made in recent years in understanding the nature of complex control systems. The approach has been to combine the mechanistic outlook of the electronic expert and servo-mechanism engineer with the organic knowledge of the biologist and neurologist into the new science of cybernetics.

This may be defined as the study of control systems in man and machine and the relation between them. In the words of Stafford Beer: 'Cybernetic systems are complex, interacting, probabilistic networks such as brains, markets, living organisms, industries, battles. Cyberneticians undertake the study of control in all these and many other contexts. How are such large systems organized? They seem to be cohesive, self regulating, and stable, yet adaptive to change and capable of learning from experience'.

From the work of cyberneticians two important control principles have emerged: one is that of error-actuated feedback, the other is homeostasis. The feedback principle can best be illustrated in one of its simplest forms, that of driving a car. The driver aims at a certain position on the road and checks after a few seconds if that position has been attained. If the difference between the desired position and the actual position is great enough an appropriate adjustment is made to the steering wheel, the new position is checked after a further few seconds, and the cycle is repeated. The significance of this operation is that the error between the actual and required position is fed back to the driver and action is taken on the size of the error. This is what is meant by error actuated feedback.

The inexperienced driver, determined to permit himself the minimum amount of wander, will take corrective action on the smallest observed deviation and will make the amount of correction equal to the error. Thus the tyro's steering wheel is continually a-wobble and, as is well known, the result of his efforts is to wander about the road more than a skilled man.

The experienced driver knows, firstly, that certain errors in position are quite random and are accidental ones due to variations in road contour or other chance causes, and might well be self-corrected at the next bump. These deviations he ignores and thus steers a smoother course than the learner. Secondly, he knows that, when a deviation is serious enough to take into account, the correction he makes should be somewhat less than the error to avoid the risk of over-correction. He thus gradually restores the vehicle to its original course. The dangers of making the feedback equal to the error are well illustrated in temperature controllers which exhibit the familiar phenomenon of 'hunting'.

Homeostasis is the property that all living organisms have of making use of error-actuated feedback to adjust their metabolism to changing environmental conditions, so that certain essential parameters remain constant. The blood temperature of a healthy reader of this book stays constant at 98.4°F whether he be reading it in tropical humidity or sub-zero frost. The homeostatic mechanism is one that itself responds to the error actuated feedback instead of relying on an outside agent such as the car driver.

The principle is clearly an important one for industry. The environment of many industrial processes is continually changing. The raw materials vary, the process conditions change, the quality of the operating workers may deteriorate. Even if nothing else alters, the plant itself is ageing and this can cause changes in the quality of the product. Few readers of this book will not have experienced the sudden appearance of new and complex problems on old-established processes. These are just symptoms of changes in the process which were not detected and rectified by subtle homeostatic procedures, but were allowed to accumulate until their presence could no longer be ignored.

The application of error actuated feedback and homeostasis to industrial operations is a difficult job. The manager of a process is not driving a car, able to see the road ahead; he is in the position a car driver would be in if he only had a glimpse of the road five miles back every few minutes or so. The analogy cannot be stretched too far obviously, but more O.R. will have to be carried out before these principles can be applied to the management function.

The approach is twofold. One way is to build the feedback and homeostasis into the organizational structure so that the appropriate observations are made and the corrections introduced by a human agency. The other is to design process machines that can do the job.

The first method offers more scope for advance on a short-term basis, and one process known to us is operating on these principles. Observations are taken on a comprehensive scale and with sufficient frequency to enable any significant process changes to be detected. The limits within which the plant personnel can make changes themselves are clearly laid down but in such a way as not to inhibit development. When changes of a certain magnitude occur, outside technical help must be invoked. In this way adequate feedback at all levels of the process operation is ensured, and the homeostatic experience of the plant operators with their knowledge of intimate detail and that of the technicians with their specialist training is utilized to the full. The use of cybernetic principles also helps in clarifying the organization aspects of process control.

Other companies have also inaugurated cybernetic schemes based on organization structure. The best known is that designed by Beer, and this too requires the collection and constant analysis of a large amount of information. Industry tends to fight shy of schemes that require a large amount of information because data collecting can be very expensive. It should be noted, however, as explained in the section on Information Theory, that the adequacy of a control system depends upon the amount of information contained in it. To confirm this, see how accurately you can drive a car by only looking at the road every two minutes. In many cases it may be more expensive not to have the information than to collect it.

The second method of advance, that of designing a machine, may overcome the problem of providing information and analysing it, because this will very largely be done by the machine itself at little or no extra cost. The design and manufacture of such a machine will of course be a very comprehensive task.

That such machines can exist has been demonstrated theoretically by Ashby, and a machine that exhibits a lot of the necessary properties is now being produced by the Solartron Group for teaching card punch operators. The machine sets the exercises for the pupil and adjusts itself to the pupil's characteristics in a cybernetic manner, concentrating on the learner's weaknesses or speeding up the exercises to the limits of the pupil's capacity.

That these machines will come there is no doubt. They will have many properties that are very desirable in control system – continuous feedback, rapid response, an ability to recognize patterns better than do human beings, the capacity to explore numerous alternatives without exhaustion, and so on. Before the machines are available, however, there is a lot that the O.R. worker can do in applying the same principles on an organizational basis so that industry can make much more effective use of the control information it has, and be encouraged to obtain further information where it is economically advantageous to do so.

One such cybernetic principle, which it is useful to expand on a little at this stage, is the Black Box principle. In cybernetics a Black Box is a system that is too complex to be understood fully in the existing state of knowledge. Most companies are Black Boxes. The economic system of this country certainly is. To attempt to understand the nature of the interrelations inside a Black Box in order to inaugurate the necessary feedback controls can be a fruitless and unrewarding task, and one in fact that had better be left unattempted, because if the system is complex enough the control may be achieved in a far simpler way.

The Black Box principle in cybernetics states that the behaviour of the complex system is discovered merely by studying the relationship between the input and the output, and not by considering what happens inside the Black Box. By studying the relationship between input and output one can often learn what changes are needed to the input to achieve a given change in output, and thus learn all that is needed to control the system.

As an example of this principle, applied in a very simple manner, a production controller was once worried about how to schedule a tool room. The nature of the work in the tool room seemed to vary considerably in size, complexity, the time taken for machining, and so on. To apply conventional production control methods would have necessitated the employment of about three or four clerks to record all the necessary information inside the Black Box.

The production controller noticed, however, that when the tool room was fully occupied it produced about forty jobs per week. This number varied somewhat of course, but the average stayed fairly constant at forty. Thus he argued that an input of forty jobs per week should keep the tool room fully occupied and ensure an output of forty jobs per week. He could also schedule the plant developments which were waiting for the tool room to complete its work on the basis of a tool room output of forty jobs per week. This simple rule proved very effective and is an illustration of how the Black Box principle in cybernetics can be used to control situations that, if gone into deeply, may seem very complex.

A further example of the Black Box principle is the treatment of mental patients. The human brain is certainly a Black Box, and while a great deal of neurological research is going on to understand the mechanism of the brain, progress in treatment is also being made by observing patients' responses to stimuli.

REFERENCES

Ashby, W.R., *An Introduction to Cybernetics*, Methuen, 1964.
Beer, S., *Cyberneties and Management*, E.U.P., 1959.

Information theory

This is akin to cybernetics and will have but brief mention in this book, because its industrial applications are as yet few. It is worth mentioning, however, because modern industry depends for its operation upon the efficiency of its internal and external communication systems. The middle manager in particular spends most of his time in communication (see Burns), and surprisingly little, perhaps too little, time in thinking and planning. It is thus most important for industry to understand the properties of its communication systems, since without this understanding they will be used inefficiently.

How often, for example, when some grave mistake has been made in a firm, sufficiently serious to warrant a post-mortem, has it been found to be due not to gross inefficiency on the part of any individual but to a failure in the communication system?

The properties of communication systems have been studied very fully by telephone engineers, and the first formal publication of results was by Shannon. He originally used the title Communication Theory, but because the notion of a quantitative measure of information was central to his theme the name Information Theory has come into use.

Shannon's results were as follows:

(1) Information cannot be transmitted at any arbitrarily great rate over a given communication system. It is possible, given all the necessary properties of a communication system, to calculate the maximum rate at which information can be transmitted.

(2) Communications made in a system are not entirely independent of one another and do not occur with a completely random distribution. In English speech for instance the letter 'e' occurs with much more frequency than the letter 'k', and we can often complete an unfinished word or sentence with a high degree of exactitude. This property, that some information is expected with a greater frequency than other information, can be used in the design of a system.

(3) There is always random interference, i.e. noise, in any communication system. This occurs in telephone speech of course, and even with written messages there is a finite probability of them going astray.

The result of Shannon can be expressed mathematically and used for the design of telephone circuits. At present they cannot readily be used for the design and improvement of business communication systems, but the time will probably come when they can be.

Even the general principles can be useful to managers, however. They must not expect information to be transmitted through their organization at great speed without errors occurring. This is a warning against the panic actions that are frequent in some organizations and often disastrous. Conversely, if a manager wishes to ensure that information is transmitted free from error, he must give plenty of time for its transmission.

For a message to be really clear and free from ambiguity it must contain a lot of apparently unnecessary and redundant information. This is because not all the information can be absorbed and thus it is necessary to put in surplus information. Not for nothing did the negro preacher say: 'I tells 'em what I'm going to tell 'em; I tell 'em; then I tells 'em what I've told 'em.'

Finally the manager must expect that information will be lost from his organization and will need to be replaced. This is well known to every librarian's filing clerk. It may seem to be due to inefficiency and mistakes, but it is an inevitable phenomenon of every information system and should be recognized as such.

There is a relationship between information theory and cybernetics. The degree of control of a system is proportional to the logarithm of the information in this system. This relationship is shown in Fig. 11.2, and it serves to emphasize what was said in the section on cybernetics, that no system can be adequately controlled without sufficient information. At present we do not know how much information is necessary to ensure an adequate degree of control, but with development of information theory our knowledge of control may improve. For further reading the books of Cherry should be consulted.

REFERENCES

Burns, T., "Management in action," *O.R.Q.*, Vol. 8, No. 1, 1957.

Cherry, C. (Ed.), Information Theory, 2nd London Conference.
Cherry, C., *On Human Communication*, Chapman and Hall, 1957.
Shannon, C.E. and Weave, W., *The Mathematical Theory of Communication*, University of Illinois, 1949.

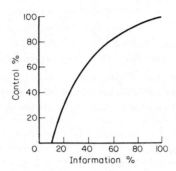

Fig. 11.2. Relationship between control and information.

Organizational planning

This is the process of determining an effective system of distribution of power and authority to various levels of human beings so that an organizational plan emerges. The plan that enables the achievement of overall organizational goals to be best achieved is the aim that is, for obvious reasons, rarely obtained. The allocation and use of power has the highest priority among all the factors that concern management, but a cold analysis of alternatives is seldom practicable.

REFERENCES

Dalton, G.W., Lawrence, P.R. and Lorsch, J.W., *Organisational Structure and Design*, Irwin-Dorsey, 1970.
Shull, Jr., F.A., Delbeiq, A.L. and Cummings, L.L., *Organisational Decision Making*, McGraw-Hill, 1970.

Process analysis

This is the study of the process(es) used for the production or service of a product in order to develop a least-cost, i.e. efficient, schedule of operation to produce outputs of acceptable quality. The analysis forms part of what has come to be known as Work Study. The normal procedure is to produce a process chart to represent graphically the sequence of activities during a series of actions and/or operations.

REFERENCES

Eary, D.F. and Johnson, G.E., *Process Engineering for Manufacturing*, Prentice-Hall, 1962.

Quality control

This is basically a quantitative aid to determining when a production process has got out of control, i.e. when certain measurements of quality become statistically unlikely to be random deviations and are likely to be due to a systematic cause. The technique provides a rapid feedback of deviations which appear non-random, giving early warning for corrective decision-taking.

REFERENCES

Moroney, M.J., *Facts from Figures*, Chapter 12, Penguin, 1951.

Break-even analysis

This provides a method for studying relationships between, for example, sales returns, fixed and variable costs, and sales volumes, in order to determine the *minimum* volume at which production becomes worthwhile, i.e. profitable. A break-even formula can be defined as:

$$V = F/(1 - R)$$

where V is the break-even sales volume, F is the total fixed costs, and R is the ratio of total variable costs to expected net sales volume.

REFERENCES

"Three applications of break-even methods in economic analysis," in *Engineering Economist*, a publication of the Engineering Economy Division, American Society for Engineering Education, No. 1, 1961.

This, by no means exhaustive, summary of quantitative management aids serves to illustrate how quantitative a subject management has now become. Literacy has always been a necessary management skill, numeracy is now equally so. For those managers whose lack of this numeracy is causing concern, the book by Battersby can be highly recommended as a crash course!

REFERENCES

Battersby, A., *Mathematics in Management*, Penguin Books, 1966.

12 Conclusion

I know why the Dodo
Has gone from land and sea
He lived Suaviter in Modo
Not Fortiter in Re!

Punch

If your purpose in reading this book was just to become acquainted with the purpose and power of Operational Research techniques, we hope that you have now gained this understanding. If you are a manager who wished to improve the performance of his company by using operational research techniques, we hope that we have shown how this may be done. If you are a young student interested to know whether operational research offers a rewarding career for you, we hope that we have conveyed some of the excitement and scope of operational research as a profession.

To the first type of reader we would just say that this monograph has not been intended as a comprehensive review of O.R. Much bigger and better books have been written, and we trust your enthusiasm has been aroused to the extent that you will go on to read these and acquaint yourself even more with the power of O.R. techniques.

To the second reader, the manager, who has decided that he should use O.R. techniques, we would now like to be presumptuous enough to offer some direct advice. You will be concerned with how to site the O.R. function, how to start it up, and how to find trained staff. The proper siting of an O.R. department in an industrial organization is most important because, unless it is in the correct location, and unless the relationship between the O.R. function and the other required functions of the organization has been clearly thought out, it is unlikely that the department will be effective.

The work of a company consists essentially of three operations: development, production, and sales. Without any one of these it will cease to exist. Any one of these operational tasks requires three factors for its accomplishment: personnel, techniques, and programmes. These are the three essential phases of work. No task can be achieved without involving a person (automatic machines not excepted since they are evolved by people), a technique, and a programme. In a company with a clear-cut organizational structure, the operating commands of development, production, and sales will be clearly differentiated and so will the staff functions of personnel, techniques, and programming.

Operational Research in general has to do with the programming function in the industry, and all the methods described in this book will be found to apply to the programming problem which is the balancing of the capacity of the company, in terms of production, financial resources, development, and sales effort, with the demands made on it by customers, so as to produce the optimum results for the shareholders and employees. Linear programming is not used for selecting personnel or for developing manufacturing techniques; it is used for optimizing the use of capacity. Queuing theory is not used for training people in metallurgical know-how; it is used for balancing demand and capacity.

The actions people take in business games are not those concerned in the personnel or technical fields; they are the actions of a programmer. Thus is O.R. concerned with programming, and the O.R. team should be responsible to the man in charge of the programming function. In a small firm he will undoubtedly be the managing director; this is unavoidable. In a small firm the O.R. team should be directly responsible to him because the managing director is probably the only man who can see the system he is in charge of in sufficient outline for the value of O.R. to be appreciated.

In a company of more than, say, 1000 employees, the managing director is likely to have delegated the programming function, and the best place for the O.R. team is therefore one step removed from him. The difficulty is that in many cases it is not clear to whom this function has been delegated.

The first task of O.R. in such a firm might well be to have the programming function clarified so that one person can be made responsible for it, to whose group the O.R. team can clearly be attached. In other situations it may be attached to the person with the greatest degree of programming responsibility. In a single factory he may be the production controller. In a company he may be one of the directors, or a general manager, or the chief accountant. In any event, the O.R. team will function more effectively if it is responsible to someone with the authority to implement schemes that improve the efficiency of the programming function.

Some O.R. teams in industry are attached to research departments or other sections such as central administration, and are there to provide a service to those who want it. This might sound very nice and genteel, and it does great credit to the personal relationships within any such organization that the O.R. team placed in this situation does a good job and gets many ideas accepted and into operation. But it says nothing for the managing director of such an organization that he allows such a practice to go on. He should not allow the efficiency of his organization in such a major field as programming to depend upon the good personal relationships of his staff.

He should clarify his organization, delegate one man for the programming task, and see that the O.R. team is responsible to him. In the absence of such clarification, O.R. work is unlikely to be fully effective and will depend for such success as it achieves on the expenditure of a lot of effort on personal persuasion.

How to start up operational research

The beginning of O.R. in an organization is a somewhat delicate task. The one thing to avoid is ballyhoo. Operational Research does not work miracles, and to herald the arrival of an O.R. man or department as if it were the management panacea is to condemn it to impotence for some considerable time.

Operational Research depends for its success on the people who must work the schemes having confidence that they will work. This applies notwithstanding the above remarks on personal relationships, because if no one else need be considered the programmer has to be, and he is usually a shrewd, able, and experienced man. People in industry are naturally happier and more efficient when working schemes that they believe in than when they sullenly follow the dictates of higher authority.

It is thus best to commence O.R. on minor problems, say the production scheduling of a single product, the purchasing of a particular type of stores, a congestion situation in a small unit, and so on. If possible, the initial tasks should be those with a high probability of success using known O.R. techniques, so that confidence can be gained in the use of these techniques and in the people using them. Big jobs need a lot of data collection and interviews with many senior executives. These are difficult to conduct effectively without experienced staff who are accepted as such.

Herrmann and Magee have adequately defined the type of problem on which it is suitable to begin O.R. In their words:

'(1) There should be an opportunity for decision between alternative courses of action.'

'(2) There should be a real possibility for quantitative study and measurement. Thus, a preliminary study to provide bases for predicting the acceptance of fabric styles had to be quickly dropped in one case because of the inability to construct within a reasonable period an adequate quantitative description of the complexities of fabric, style, pattern, and colour.'

'(3) It should be possible to collect data. In one case, analysis of accounts receivable for the previous two years yielded the key to a knotty marketing problem. But, in another case, a study of maintenance problems was found to be uneconomical because of the lack of available records showing maintenance breakdown histories on equipment.'

'(4) It should be possible to evaluate results readily. In other words, the problem should not be so large that it is indefinite; there should be some specific aspect which lends itself to solution. Neither the analyst nor the most enthusiastic executive can expect O.R. activities to be supported on the basis of faith alone.'

'The final choice is best made in co-operation with the research team. Executives have found it useful to map out the general area in advance; the research group can then comment on those aspects which are most amenable to study, to clear formulation of the problem, and to likelihood of progress with reasonable effort. On this basis a specific problem can be selected which meets the requirements both of the executive (for importance and use) and of the research group (for suitability of existing data for quantitative study).'

'Much frustration and dissatisfaction can be avoided when the research team and the executives keep in mind each other's needs. The research team must formulate a sufficiently understandable statement of the problem and method of attack to provide the executives with confidence in giving support. The executives, in turn, must recognize that, in research, advance specifications for a detailed programme including scope and goals are frequently difficult and usually meaningless; they must provide the group with access to the necessary data and people, and they must maintain contact with the work, guiding and redirecting it along the lines of greatest value as it develops.'

Once O.R. has proved itself on simple tasks, wider and wider problems can be tacked until O.R. is being fruitfully employed on programming problems affecting the whole of the company's operations.

This need not necessarily apply, of course, where an outside consultant is being employed to carry out an O.R. investigation. The size of job to be tackled by him must clearly depend upon the employer's assessment of his capabilities and a knowledge of the kind of job he has done for other firms.

It is not too difficult to find competent Operational Research people. A good guide to salaries (in Great Britain) is the scales provided by the administrative branch of the U.K. Civil Service. It is possible to start up an O.R. department by attracting an experienced O.R. investigaror who now wishes to lead his own team, and let him build up the department from within the company as the need for it is demonstrated.

Another way is to call in an outside firm of consultants to tackle particular jobs and to train either the employing company's existing staff, or specially selected staff, in O.R. techniques.

Yet a third way is to find a member of your staff who is interested in O.R., and seems capable of being good at it, and to send him away to be trained at one of the recognized courses recommended by the U.K. Operational Research Society. On his return from these courses he may be supported in his first few tasks by an outside consulting organization.

The essential thing throughout all these steps in starting up your own O.R. section is for it to have your complete support. Nothing ever succeeds in a company, certainly nothing that can eventually cause such radical changes in attitude as an O.R. investigation, without it having the full committed support of the chief executive. If you are unconvinced at this stage that O.R. techniques warrant such support from you, we have certainly failed in our task this far, but would recommend that you go on an Operational Research course yourself. Whether it convinces you of the need for Operational Research or not, it will certainly widen your ideas of your management function, and this may eventually lead to your using O.R. in a modest sense by initially employing outside consultants, and then, after their success, setting up your own function in the proper manner. We wish you luck in the interests of the survival of your company.

To the third of our readers, the student who is wondering about an O.R. career, we would recommend you to join the Operational Research Society in your own country, and to talk to some of its practitioners just above your own age.

It is a young profession; more than half of its members are under 30 years old, with high academic standards. Over 90% have a degree, and nearly 40% a postgraduate qualification of some sort. It is also a profession that is becoming more professional. Increasingly the postgraduate qualification gained is in Operational Research and not the subject in which the graduate first studied.

Of the work performed by members of the O.R. Society, mathematics heads the list, followed by computer simulation. The average time between promotions is only two years; the average time with an employer is under four years. It is a profession that can lead to high managerial positions in mid-career.

Having, we hope, given satisfactory, if gratuitous, advice to our three classes of reader, we would now just like to finish with a few general observations about the state of Operational Research at the beginning of its fourth decade of serious application in industry.

When the first edition of this book appeared in 1962, Operational Research was at the beginning of a great boom in industrial application. It is now through that stage and has, in middle age as it were, settled down into an appropriate groove. Very many large companies no longer think of their Operational Research teams as being, in a sense, pioneering; they are a settled part of the industrial structure.

All the big oil and chemical companies, most steel firms, big department stores, local authorities, and central government use O.R. techniques as a matter of course. It has influenced our everyday lives, possibly not always for the better it seems! Anyone who has ever received a *Readers Digest* leaflet has been selected as a result of a linear programme.

Many O.R. teams have recognized that the search for truly optimal solutions, however desirable they may be, and by whatever techniques may have been available, is somewhat of an illusion. In many cases all that there is time to find are solutions which are acceptable, because so much time has often to be spent by managers in making sure that the solutions actually work in practice. But this is not to mean that other optimal solutions may not be available to be used at some time in the future. Managers with experienced O.R. teams will by now have had confidence in them, and should begin to consider involving them in really long-term, strategic planning.

As was emphasized in the Preface, many complex situations can sometimes be controlled by quite simple rules. The main purpose of the chief executive, especially of a large organization, is to understand how to manipulate the fortunes of his organization by fairly simple procedures. Many of the great simplifying laws of physics apply, with modifications, to human situations. Possibly the most striking is the relationship between Boyle's Law, which relates the pressure and volume of a gas, and Parkinson's First Law, which relates the pressure and volume of work. Although Parkinson's Laws were proposed in a humorous context, they have a surprising degree of validity and are a very good example of shrewd observation, leading to useful concepts for administrative purposes.

Another great physical principle which could be applied to the administrative field is Le Chatelier's principle which states that when a system is subject to constraints it acts in such a way as to minimize the effects of those constraints upon the system. If only those who formulated our taxation laws could thoroughly understand how Le Chatelier's principle applies to the response to changes in taxation, we may find that taxation could be modified so as to encourage effort instead of suppressing it.

The behaviour of human beings in very complex situations is subject to some surprisingly simple statistical laws. In Britain about 20 people a day are killed on the roads. Nobody can predict at the beginning of each day who will die or how, but at the end of each day about 20 people have gone. This is a property of the road system and how it is used. We know how to make roads safer, and often do so, but to bring the deaths down to zero for a day would be prohibitively expensive because, after all, society does place a financial value on human life which in terms of road safety is surprisingly low.

To deny that human behaviour in complex situations is not subject to simple laws is therefore to deny the teachings of history. Keynesian thought has dominated economic thinking since Bretton Woods. What was missed from his formulation was the destructive power of inflation powered by public finance. Adam Smith's *The Wealth of Nations* conditioned economic policies for two centuries before Keynes. Unpredicted by him was the political power of working people which makes inflation preferable to unemployment long before the flash point of revolution is reached.

We are now beginning to grasp that, when public expenditure reaches some point above 50% of GNP, not only is inflation difficult to control but democracy is in danger also.

The understanding of phenomena that are needed to tackle these very big problems is very big itself. Its exploration by O.R. methods is beyond the scope of this book but a relevant book has been written by Stafford Beer entitled *Decision and Control.*

If we have encouraged any chief executive or even a major politician or civil servant to proceed to read this book, and to begin seriously to understand how the proper use of Operational Research concepts could change the character of the management of his entire command, then we shall have achieved our final purpose in writing this book.

REFERENCES

Beer, S., *Decisions and Control – The Meaning of Operational Research and Management Cybernetics*, Wiley, New York, 1966.
Hermann, C.F. and Magee, J.F., "Operations Research for Management," *Harvard Business Review*, July-August 1953, p. 100.
Parkinson, C. Northcote, *Parkinson's Law or the Pursuit of Progress*, John Murray, London, 1958.

Name Index

201

General Index